BASIC/NOT BORING
LANGUAGE SKILLS

FOURTH GRADE BOOK OF LANGUAGE TESTS

Series Concept & Development
by Imogene Forte & Marjorie Frank

Illustrations by Kathleen Bullock

Incentive Publications, Inc.
Nashville, Tennessee

About the cover:
Bound resist, or tie dye, is the most ancient known method of fabric surface design. The brilliance of the basic tie dye design on this cover reflects the possibilities that emerge from the mastery of basic skills.

Cover art by Mary Patricia Deprez, dba Tye Dye Mary®
Cover design by Marta Drayton and Joe Shibley
Edited by Angela Reiner

ISBN 0-86530-462-9

Copyright ©2000 by Incentive Publications, Inc., Nashville, TN. All rights reserved. No part of this publication may be reproduced, stored in a retrieval system, or transmitted in any form or by any means (electronic, mechanical, photocopying, recording, or otherwise) without written permission from Incentive Publications, Inc., with the exception below.

Pages labeled with the statement ©**2000 by Incentive Publications, Inc., Nashville, TN** are intended for reproduction. Permission is hereby granted to the purchaser of one copy of **BASIC/NOT BORING FOURTH GRADE BOOK OF LANGUAGE TESTS** to reproduce these pages in sufficient quantities for meeting the purchaser's own classroom needs only.

PRINTED IN THE UNITED STATES OF AMERICA
www.incentivepublications.com

TABLE OF CONTENTS

Inside the Fourth Grade Book of Language Tests 7
How to Use the Fourth Grade Book of Language Tests 8

READING **10**
Reading Skills Checklists 10
Test # 1: Word Meanings 12
Test # 2: Literal Comprehension 18
Test # 3: Inferential & Evaluative Comprehension 24
Test # 4: Literature Skills 30

WRITING **36**
Writing Skills Checklists 36
Test # 1: Word Choice & Word Use 38
Test # 2: Forms & Techniques 40
Test # 3: Content & Organization 44
Test # 4: Editing 48
Test # 5: Writing Process 52

GRAMMAR & USAGE **60**
Grammar & Usage Skills Checklists 60
Test # 1: Parts of Speech 62
Test # 2: Sentences 66
Test # 3: Punctuation & Capitalization 68
Test # 4: Language Usage 72

WORDS & VOCABULARY SKILLS **76**
Words & Vocabulary Skills Checklists 76
Test # 1: Word Parts 78
Test # 2: Vocabulary Word Meanings 80
Test # 3: Confusing Words 84

STUDY & RESEARCH SKILLS **88**
    Study & Research Skills Checklists 88
    Test # 1: Dictionary & Encyclopedia Skills 90
    Test # 2: Reference & Information Skills 94
    Test # 3: Library Skills 100
    Test # 4: Study Skills 102

SPELLING **104**
    Spelling Skills Checklists 104
    Test # 1: Rules & Rule-Breakers 106
    Test # 2: Spelling with Word Parts 108
    Test # 3: Confusing & Tricky Words 110
    Test # 4: Correcting Spelling Errors 112

KEEPING TRACK OF SKILLS **117**
    Student Progress Record Form, Language 118
    Class Progress Record
        (Reading, Writing, Grammar & Usage) 119
    Class Progress Record
        (Words & Vocabulary, Study & Research, Spelling) 120
    Good Skill Sharpeners for Language Arts 121

SCORING GUIDES & ANSWER KEYS **123**
    Reading Answer Keys 124
    Writing Answer Keys 126
    Writing Process Scoring Guide 128
    Grammar & Usage Answer Keys 130
    Words & Vocabulary Skills Answer Keys 134
    Study & Research Skills Answer Keys 137
    Spelling Answer Keys 140

INSIDE THE
FOURTH GRADE BOOK OF LANGUAGE TESTS

"I wish I had a convenient, fast way to assess basic skills and standards."

"If only I had a way to find out what my students already know about language!"

"If only I had a good way to find out what my students have learned!"

"How can I tell if my students are ready for state assessments?"

"It takes too long to create my own tests on the units I teach."

"The tests that come with my textbooks are too long and too dull."

"I need tests that cover all the skills on a topic—not just a few here and there."

This is what teachers tell us about their needs for testing materials. If you, too, are looking for quality, convenient materials that will help you gauge how well students are moving along towards mastering basic skills and standards—look no further. This is a book of tests such as you've never seen before! It's everything you've wanted in a group of ready-made assessments for 4th graders.

- The tests are student-friendly. One glance through the book and you will see why. Students will be surprised that it's a test at all! The pages are inviting and fun. A clever cat and his many rat friends tumble over the pages, leading students through language questions and problems. Your students will not groan when you pass out these tests. They'll want to stick with them all the way to the end to see which character is holding the STOP sign this time!

- The tests are serious. Do not be fooled by the catchy characters and visual appeal! These are serious, thorough assessments of basic content. As a part of the BASIC/Not Boring Skills Series, they give broad coverage of skills with a flair that makes them favorites of teachers and kids.

- The tests cover all the basic skill areas for language. There are 24 tests within 6 areas: reading, writing, grammar & usage, vocabulary & word skills, study & research skills, and spelling.

- The tests are ready to use. In convenient and manageable sizes of 2, 4, or 6 pages in length, each test covers a skill area (such as "parts of speech" or "correcting spelling errors") that should be assessed. Just give the pages to an individual student, or make copies for the entire class. Answer keys (included in back) are easy to find and easy to use.

- Skills are clearly identified. You can see exactly which skills are tested by reviewing the list of skills provided with each group of tests.

HOW TO USE THE
FOURTH GRADE BOOK OF LANGUAGE TESTS

Each test can be used in many different ways. Here are a few:
- as a pre-test to see what a student knows or can do on a certain language topic
- as a post-test to find out how well students have mastered a content or skill area
- as a review to check up on student mastery of standards or readiness for state assessments
- as a survey to provide direction for your present or future instruction
- as an instructional tool to guide students through a review of a lesson
- with one student in an assessment or tutorial setting
- with a small group of students for assessment or instruction
- with a whole class for end-of-unit assessment

The *Fourth Grade Book of Language Tests* provides you with tools for using the tests effectively and keeping track of how students are progressing on skills or standards:

- **24 Tests on the Topics You Need:** These are grouped according to broad topics within language. Each large grouping has three or more sub-tests. Tests are clearly labeled with subject area and specific topic.

- **Skills Checklists Correlated to Test Items:** At the beginning of each group of tests, you'll find a list of the skills covered. (For instance, pages 10 and 11 hold lists of skills for the four reading tests.) Each skill is matched with the exact test items assessing that skill. If a student misses an item on the test, you'll know exactly which skill needs sharpening.

- **Student Progress Records:** Page 118 holds a reproducible form that can be used to track individual student achievement on all the tests in this book. Make a copy of this form for each student, and record the student's test scores and areas of instructional need.

- **Class Progress Records:** Pages 119–120 hold reproducible forms for keeping track of a whole class. You can record the dates that tests are given, and keep comments about what you learned from that test as well as notes for further instructional needs.

- **Reference for Skill-Sharpening Activities:** Page 121 describes the BASIC/Not Boring Skills Series, a program of appealing exercises designed to teach, strengthen, and reinforce basic language skills and content. The skills covered in these books are correlated to national curriculum standards and the standards for many states.

  - **Scoring Guide for Performance Test:** A performance test is given for writing. For a complete scoring guide that assesses student performance on this test, see pages 128–129.

  - **Answer Keys:** An easy-to-use answer key is provided for each of the 24 language tests. (See pages 124–143.)

THE FOURTH GRADE LANGUAGE TESTS

Reading Skills Checklists 10–11
    4 Reading Tests 12–35
Writing Skills Checklists 36–37
    5 Writing Tests 38–59
Grammar & Usage Skills Checklists 60–61
    4 Grammar & Usage Tests 62–75
Words & Vocabulary Skills Checklists 76–77
    3 Words & Vocabulary Skills Tests 78–87
Study & Research Skills Checklists 88–89
    4 Study & Research Skills Tests 90–103
Spelling Skills Checklists 104–105
    4 Spelling Skills Tests 106–116

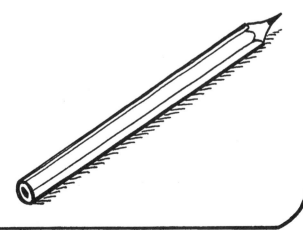

Reading Skills Checklists

Reading Test # 1:

WORD MEANINGS

Test Location: pages 12–17

Skill	Test Item
Determine word meaning from context	1–5
Determine meaning of phrases from context	6–9
Recognize and use synonyms	10–13
Recognize and use antonyms	14–17
Choose the correct word for the context of a passage	18–20
Use knowledge of prefixes to determine word meaning	21–26
Use knowledge of suffixes to determine word meaning	27–32
Use knowledge of root meanings to determine word meaning	33–40
Considering the context of a word, choose the correct meaning of a word with multiple meanings	41–42
Explain literal meaning of idioms	43–50

Reading Test # 2:

LITERAL COMPREHENSION

Test Location: pages 18–23

Skill	Test Item
Identify literal main ideas	1–2
Choose the best title for a selection	3
Identify details that support an idea or point of view	4–6
Gain information from titles, headlines, or captions	7–10
Determine sequence of events in a passage	11–12
Read to find details and information	4–6, 11–12, 13–18
Make use of graphics to gain understanding of a text	19–22
Read to follow directions	23
Read to find information in a table of contents, glossary, or index	24–30

Reading Test # 3:

INFERENTIAL & EVALUATIVE COMPREHENSION

Test Location: pages 24–29

Skill	Test Item
Identify implied main ideas	1, 2, 5
Determine the author's purpose or bias	6, 9
Identify cause-effect relationships	10–11
Distinguish between fact and opinion	12–14
Use information gained from a text to make inferences	7, 8, 15–18
Use information gained from a text to make predictions	19, 27
Make generalizations based on material read	20, 21, 25–27
Draw logical conclusions from a written text	3, 25
Evaluate ideas, conclusions, or opinions from a text	22, 23, 24
Read to interpret charts, graphs, and tables	25–30

Reading Test # 4:

LITERATURE SKILLS

Test Location: pages 30–35

Skill	Test Item
Identify different forms of literature; recognize characteristics of different literary forms (genres)	1, 7, 31, 38–45
Identify plot, setting, and characters of a piece of literature	2–4, 6, 32, 33
Identify and analyze characteristics of different characters	5
Identify main and supporting characters	2, 3, 33
Identify other elements (theme, mood) of a piece of literature	8, 9, 34
Recognize effective use of words and phrases to accomplish a purpose in the writing	10, 11, 15, 16
Identify literary devices and their effects (alliteration, simile, metaphor, rhyme, rhythm, repetition, puns, personification, idioms, hyperbole, imagery)	10, 12–14, 18–30
Identify the author's purpose	17, 36
Identify the author's bias or feelings about the subject	35, 37

Subject, Test #1

WORD MEANINGS

Name _____ Possible Correct Answers: 50

Date _____ Your Correct Answers: _____

1. Caspian tried to be punctual every day, but he always arrived late for practice.
   In this sentence, **punctual** means:
   a. careful.
   b. helpful.
   c. on time.
   d. responsible.

2. To augment his bank account, Caspian got a job delivering newspapers.
   In this sentence, **augment** means:
   a. keep track of.
   b. add to.
   c. take away from.
   d. up-to-date.

3. The coach berated the team members for missing practice four times.
   In this sentence, **berated** means:
   a. scolded.
   b. praised.
   c. complimented.
   d. rewarded.

4. This note is so illegible that I cannot possibly read it, no matter how hard I try to figure it out.
   In this sentence, **illegible** means:
   a. disturbing.
   b. unreadable.
   c. torn.
   d. exciting.

5. Aunt Maggie sent her boisterous nieces home because her ears hurt and she was afraid her furniture would be destroyed.
   In this sentence, **boisterous** means:
   a. rowdy and noisy.
   b. mean.
   c. favorite.
   d. naughty.

Read the story below.

It was almost dark when the tired hikers arrived at their camping spot. "I'll pitch the tent," said Elmo. "It'll be a snap."

"Why don't I cook up a mountain of pancakes?" suggested Reggie. "Let's get some firewood," said Gigi, as she headed into the woods.

Just as she and Rufus entered the woods, Gigi heard a sound that made her heart leap. It was a long, low growl. She turned to face a large brown bear, looming above her.

As Gigi raced back into the campsite, Reggie did some fast thinking. He set a plate of steaming pancakes loaded with syrup right in the path of the bear. The bear stopped, sat down, and happily gobbled up the pancakes. Then he wandered lazily away.

"Whew!" they all exclaimed. "We got out of that one by the skin of our teeth!"

6. When Elmo says, **"I'll pitch the tent. It'll be a snap!"** he means:
   a. "I'll snap the tent together."
   b. "It will be easy to set up the tent."
   c. "I'll throw the tent away."
   d. "The tent will make a snapping sound."

7. When Reggie suggests cooking **"a mountain of pancakes,"** he means:
   a. he will cook pancakes shaped like a mountain.
   b. he will cook pancakes on the mountain.
   c. he will use a special batter for the pancakes.
   d. he will cook a lot of pancakes.

8. When the story says Gigi heard a sound that **"made her heart leap,"** it means:
   a. her heart moved inside her body.
   b. her heart hurt.
   c. the sound scared her.
   d. the sound made her happy.

9. When the campers said that they **"got out of that one by the skin of our teeth,"** they meant that:
   a. they narrowly missed being attacked by the bear.
   b. they had skin on their teeth.
   c. they used their teeth to help them escape from the bear.
   d. they got the skin off their teeth.

Word Meanings

Read the sign.

EAST BEACH DIVE CENTER
- Proceed to information booth.
- Acquire a permit before diving.
- Annual diving fee—$20
- DO NOT DIVE WHEN DROWSY.
- Descend slowly on all dives.
- Feeding fish is strictly forbidden.
- Don't miss the incredible underwater wonders.
- Use suitable equipment.
- West Entrance is temporarily closed.

On the sign find a **synonym** for each of these words:

10. unbelievable _____
11. get _____
12. yearly _____
13. appropriate _____

On the sign find an **antonym** (opposite) for each of these words:

14. hastily _____
15. stop _____
16. permitted _____
17. permanently _____

Choose the correct word for each sentence.

18. Please _____ from annoying the fish.
   a. refuse   c. reflect
   b. refrain   d. restrain

19. The divers _____ that the rough waves made them sick.
   a. bragged   c. wished
   b. decided   d. complained

20. To be safe, swimmers should make sure all their life vests are properly _____.
   a. deflated   c. inflated
   b. defective   d. inverted

Name _____

Choose the correct meaning for each word. Pay attention to the **prefixes**.

21. **rewritten**
    a. written wrong
    b. written again
    c. partly written
    d. not written

22. **foresee**
    a. see four things
    b. see wrongly
    c. see ahead
    d. not see

23. **cooperate**
    a. operate again
    b. operate together
    c. operate between
    d. operate before

24. **improper**
    a. not proper
    b. partly proper
    c. more proper
    d. proper afterwards

25. **preview**
    a. view again
    b. not view
    c. view afterwards
    d. view before

26. **interstate**
    a. in the middle of states
    b. within a state
    c. between states
    d. against the state

Choose the correct meaning for each word. Pay attention to the **suffixes**.

27. **friendless**
    a. in a friendly way
    b. not friendly
    c. without friends
    d. with friends

28. **dangerous**
    a. without danger
    b. like danger
    c. toward danger
    d. full of danger

29. **lovable**
    a. able to be loved
    b. without love
    c. full of love
    d. one who loves

30. **powerful**
    a. toward power
    b. taking away power
    c. full of power
    d. away from power

31. **detective**
    a. the act of detecting
    b. someone who detects
    c. able to be detected
    d. unable to be detected

32. **grumpiness**
    a. not grumpy
    b. someone who is grumpy
    c. able to be grumpy
    d. the condition of being grumpy

Name _____ 15

Word Meanings

Use your knowledge of the meanings of root words to answer the questions. Choose words from Caspian's chart. Write the word on the line.

33. Which word has a root that means **sun**?
_____

34. Which word has a root that means **see**?
_____

35. Which word has a root that means **flower**?
_____

36. Which word has a root that means **earth**?
_____

37. Which word has a root that means **water**?
_____

38. Which word has a root that means **foot**?
_____

39. Which word has a root that means **small**?
_____

40. Which word has a root meaning **sound**?
_____

floral
pedestrian
fraction
microscope
geography
solar
telephone
visible
aquarium

Name _____

Fourth Grade Book of Language Tests

41. **It was so nice for you to help me out of that jam.**
    In this sentence, the word **jam** means:
    a. to pack in until something is overfilled.
    b. to crush between two surfaces.
    c. a preserve made from fruit.
    d. to squeeze into a tight place.
    e. a difficult or troublesome situation.

42. **Rhoda's cousin can't come to the game because she has a bad case of measles.**
    In this sentence, the word **case** means:
    a. a container or piece of luggage.
    b. an occurrence of a disease.
    c. a set of reasons.
    d. a covering for a pillow.
    e. a legal action taken to court.

Write the letter of the **idiom** that matches each definition.

A. Do it on the double.
B. You're in the doghouse.
C. You're driving me up a wall.
D. Drop me a line.
E. Don't horse around.
F. Don't try to worm your way out of it!
G. You're pulling my leg.
H. HOLD YOUR HORSES!

_____ 43. Be patient.

_____ 44. You're in trouble.

_____ 45. You're annoying me.

_____ 46. Write me a letter.

_____ 47. You're teasing me.

_____ 48. Do it right away.

_____ 49. You can't avoid doing it.

_____ 50. Don't fool around.

LITERAL COMPREHENSION

Name _____ Possible Correct Answers: 30

Date _____ Your Correct Answers: _____

1. Rufus is one of the few high-wire performers in the world. He holds the record for the longest and highest high-wire walk by a rat. He also holds the world record for spending the longest time on a high-wire—12 days and nights. This daring rat has performed on a 1000-foot long wire strung between two skyscrapers. The wire was 1100 feet above the ground. Rufus used a balancing stick for all of his performances. He never uses a safety net.

   What is the main idea of this paragraph?
   a. Rufus does not use a safety net.
   b. There are not many high wire walkers in the world.
   c. Rufus is a brave, record-holding high wire walker.
   d. Rufus performed 1100 feet above the ground.

2. Sky surfing—exciting to watch but difficult and dangerous to perform. Sky surfers do daring flips, rolls, and spins while they freefall through the air at high speeds. Even some of the most experienced sky surfers have suffered fatal accidents from this extreme sport.

   What is the main idea of this paragraph?
   a. Sky surfers perform cool tricks.
   b. Sky surfing is exciting, but dangerous.
   c. Many sky surfers have fatal accidents.
   d. Sky surfers fall through the air at high speeds.

Every year, thousands of forest fires turn green forests into blazing walls of flames and smoke. Firefighters tackle these blazes by trying to cool and contain the fires. They drop large amounts of water and chemicals to cool the fire. When the heat of the fire turns the water to steam, the moisture cuts down the oxygen in the air. This also helps to cool the fire.

Firefighters contain the fire by setting smaller fires around the edges. The small fires burn up the grass, small trees, and other fuel so the big fire has nothing left to burn when it reaches these edges. This helps to stop the fire.

Some firefighters parachute into the scene of a fire to help contain it. They are called smokejumpers. They jump from airplanes into the fire area to clear a path around the blaze. They may also put out small fires before they get too big. They can get to the fire faster than crews that must travel on ground. They work to contain the fire until the ground crews arrive.

3. The best title for this passage is:
   a. *Forest Fires Destroy Thousands of Trees*
   b. *The Dangers of Forest Fires*
   c. *Cooling and Containing Forest Fires*
   d. *Smokejumping: A Dangerous Job*

4. The water and chemicals:
   a. burn up the fuel around the fire's edges.
   b. cool the fire.
   c. turn the fire into a blazing wall.
   d. put out the smallest fires.

5. What can smokejumpers do that ground crews cannot?
   a. Clear a path around the blaze.
   b. Put out small fires.
   c. Get to the fire quickly.
   d. Contain the fire.

6. What is not told in the passage?
   a. what smokejumpers are
   b. how dangerous a smokejumper's job is
   c. why firefighters set small fires
   d. how steam cools down a fire

Literal Comprehension

A. Portland Gazette, March 2, 1998
IOWA WOMAN RESCUED IN MT. HOOD AVALANCHE

B. Burr Oaks News, July 18, 1997
Lost Diamond Found in Mayor's Burrito

C. Pawchuck Daily Tidings, December 10, 1999
Local Couple Wins National Bathtub Race

Vine Hill Tribune, September 12, 1998
DINOSAUR BONES DISCOVERED NEAR CITY HALL

7. Which event happened before the avalanche?

8. What was discovered in the month of September?

9. What was the home town of the bathtub racers?

10. Where was the diamond found?

The Big Race

Rico and Reggie entered the Ultimate Rat Race. The rats began the race with a fast climb up and down a 2000-foot mountain of bumpy trash. Next, they paddled a raft down a rushing stream for 3 miles. They then dove off the raft and swam back upstream for 3 miles. After that, they dried off and raced up and down a 30-foot flagpole ten times. Then they worked together to chew through a 10-inch thick rope. At the end, they were so tired that they slept right through the award ceremony.

11. Which happened third in the race?
    a. They climbed the mountain.
    b. They dove off the raft.
    c. They chewed through the rope.
    d. They paddled the raft.

12. Which happened after the flagpole climb?
    a. The rats paddled the raft down the stream.
    b. The rats entered the race.
    c. The rats chewed through rope.
    d. The rats climbed the mountain.

The Cat's Meow Café

SPECIAL BREAKFASTS

Yummy Cakes $1.80
6 large pancakes dripping with maple syrup

Scrambled Eggs & Cheese *with bacon* $3.80
Served with toast and jelly

Casper's Special $4.00
Shredded hash browns smothered in melted cheese
Served with toast and jelly

Grilled Ham & Fried Eggs $2.50
With fruit slices and toast

BREADS & PASTRIES

Cat's Paw Pastries *with chocolate icing* $2.00

Warm Pumpkin Bread *with raspberry cream* $1.50

Blackberry & Walnut Muffins *with butter* $1.50

Cheese & Bacon Muffins *with cream cheese* $1.50

Cream Cheese Muffins *with orange icing* $1.50

Onion & Cheese Bagels *with peach jam* $2.75

Raspberry Scones *with cream cheese* $1.50

---

13. Poor Rennie Rat is allergic to cheese. How many items on the menu should he avoid? _____

14. Which breakfast comes with fruit? _____

15. How much will Rennie pay for pancakes and a bagel? _____

16. What is the topping on a Cat's Paw Pastry? _____

17. How many different kinds of muffins are served? _____

18. How many breakfast items come with toast? _____

Literal Comprehension

Rhoda and some friends went to Diamond Island to search for the buried diamonds. They used the map and the mysterious letter.

Use the map and letter to answer the questions.

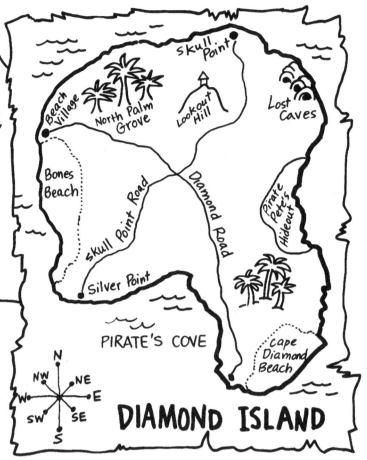

Diamond Island is 3 miles wide and 4 miles from top to bottom. From Pirate's Cove, follow Skull Point Road. Where the road meets Diamond Road, head straight north to Lookout Hill. From Lookout Hill, walk straight east toward Lost Caves. At the southern edge of lost caves, begin digging. You will find Pirate Pete's treasure chest of diamonds four feet below the surface of the sand.

19. Can you get to Pirate Pete's Hideout by road? _____

20. Which is closest to Lookout Hill?
    a. Pirate's Cove
    b. Pirate Pete's Hideout
    c. Cape Diamond Beach
    d. North Palm Grove

21. Which direction would you walk to get to Bones Beach from Skull Point? (Circle one.)

    N   S   NW   W
    NE   SE   SW   E

22. Could the distance from Lost Caves to Cape Diamond Beach be 15 miles? _____

23. Where is the treasure? Follow the directions on the letter to find the treasure.
    Draw a heavy line to follow the path that the letter describes.
    Draw a large **X** at the place where the searchers should dig for the diamonds.

Use this glossary page to answer the questions below.

SKATEBOARD TRICKS, Glossary

Backside Trick   Tail Grab

Backside Trick – Skater turns so that toes face the inside of the turn

Cab – Skater spins 360° without grabbing onto the skateboard

540 – Skater jumps in the air and spins 540° with the skateboard

Frontside Trick – Skater turns so that heels face the inside of the turn

Half Cab – Skater spins 180° without grabbing onto the skateboard

Goofy Foot Stance – Right foot is placed on the front end of the board

Halfpipe – Skating surface with a rounded basin and two vertical sides, looking much like a big **U**

Heel Flip – Skater kicks front foot forward and spins skateboard around

Indy Air – Skater jumps backside and grabs the front rail of the skateboard with back hand

Lean Air – Skater jumps frontside and grabs back rail of the skateboard with front hand

McTwist – Skater does a 540 with an inverted twist

Nose Grab – Skater jumps and grabs the front tip of the skateboard with either hand

Regular Foot Stance – Left foot is placed on the front end of the board

Stale Fish – Skater jumps forward and grabs the back rail with back hand

Slob – Skater jumps frontside and grabs the front rail of the skateboard with front hand

Tail Grab – Skater jumps and grabs the tail of the skateboard with either hand

24. Which hand does the skateboarder use to grab the rail of the skateboard in a **Stale Fish** and an **Indy Air**? _____

25. Which part of the skateboard is grabbed in a **Nose Grab**? _____

26. Which foot is on the front of the skateboard in a **Goofy Foot Stance**? _____

27. Which trick makes the greater turn: a **Half Cab** or a **540**? _____

28. What rail does the skateboarder grab in a **Slob**? _____

29. In which trick does the skater spin more: a **Cab** or a **McTwist**? _____

30. What is a **Halfpipe**? _____

Name _____

Reading Test #3

INFERENTIAL & EVALUATIVE COMPREHENSION

Name _____ Possible Correct Answers: 30

Date _____ Your Correct Answers: _____

Things Green

Green is broccoli and snakes,
Eating pickles and playing golf.
A visit to the dentist is green.
Green is the creaking of a fat bullfrog,
The smell of newly-mown grass,
And the taste of moldy cottage cheese.
Green drips slime on a slug, making
  it sticky.
Green is music, and a nap in the shade.
Getting the flu is green.
Green is the feeling you get when your
  best friend moves away.

Thomas G., Grade 5

1. The main idea of this passage is:
    a. Many things look green.
    b. Green is an unpleasant color.
    c. Critters and bad feelings are green.
    d. Sounds, sights, tastes, smells, and feelings can be green.
    e. Green is slimy.

On a trip across the Caribbean Sea, Rufus watched for sea creatures. He kept a list of every interesting creature he saw. His list had dolphins, sharks, stingrays, lobsters, and mermaids. Yes! Rufus is sure he saw several mermaids. They had long hair and long, scaly tails. He drew pictures of the mermaids he saw. What an imagination Rufus has!

2. What is the main idea of this story?
    a. Rufus believes he saw mermaids on his trip.
    b. Rufus drew pictures of mermaids.
    c. Rufus took a wonderful trip in the Caribbean Sea.

3. From the story, you can conclude that:
    a. Rufus was teasing when he said that he saw mermaids.
    b. Rufus really believed he saw mermaids.
    c. Rufus probably did not see any sea creatures.

4. Which is probably true about this story?
    a. The author saw the mermaids, too.
    b. The author does not believe Rufus saw mermaids.
    c. The author is amazed that Rufus saw mermaids.

Read this letter. Then answer the questions.

> Dear Felix,
>
> I know you have planned to come next week for a nice beach vacation. I need to tell you about our weather. We have been told that Hurricane Henry is heading for our coast. You may know that a hurricane is a strong tropical storm that gathers warm, wet air over the ocean. Some hurricanes have winds of more than 100 miles per hour. These winds cause terrible damage when they hit the shore. You never know what can happen in hurricane season. We are not sure if the hurricane will hit Miami, but it could. I know that you are afraid of high winds anyway. I thought you should be aware that there is a chance Hurricane Henry might pay us a visit next week.
>
> Sincerely,
> Cousin Elmo

5. The main point that the letter-writer makes is:
   a. Hurricanes are very dangerous.
   b. Hurricanes are tropical storms.
   c. A hurricane may hit Miami next week.
   d. Cousin Felix does not like winds.

6. What is the letter-writer's purpose?
   a. to warn people about the dangers of hurricanes
   b. to encourage Felix to re-think his vacation plans
   c. to teach Felix something about hurricanes
   d. to tell Felix to bring clothes for rain

7. From this letter, you can infer that:
   a. Elmo probably thinks Felix should not come to Miami next week.
   b. Elmo wants Felix to come anyway.
   c. Elmo does not like Felix.
   d. Felix likes hurricanes.

8. From this letter, you can infer that:
   a. Weather forecasters are sure the hurricane will hit Miami.
   b. Forecasters are not sure if Hurricane Henry will hit Miami.
   c. Hurricane Henry has winds of over 100 miles per hour.

Inferential & Evaluative Comprehension

I rode *The Corkscrew* five times today. It is the most thrilling rollercoaster in the world. You are probably wondering how people can ride an upside-down coaster without falling out. Here's how. Riders wear safety harnesses, but that is not the main thing that keeps them in the coaster. Inertia and speed keep riders in their seats. When an object is set in motion by a force, it continues moving in that direction until something stops it. This is called inertia. The force of inertia is stronger than the gravity pulling down. When the cars go upside down, the speed of the rollercoaster and the inertia keeps the cars and riders moving forward along the track instead of falling down toward the ground. Being upside down on *The Corkscrew* is a great feeling. Everyone will want to try it.

9. The purpose of this passage is:
   a. to invite people to ride The Corkscrew
   b. to help people who are afraid of rollercoasters
   c. to explain why riders don't fall out of a roller coaster that goes upside down
   d. to compare different rollercoasters to The Corkscrew

10. In this pair of sentences, one sentence tells a cause. The other tells the effect. Mark each sentence **C (cause)** or **E (effect)**.
    ____ a. The writer was thrilled about The Corkscrew.
    ____ b. The writer just rode The Corkscrew five times.

11. In this pair of sentences, one sentence tells a cause. The other tells the effect. Mark each sentence **C (cause)** or **E (effect)**.
    ____ a. Riders did not fall out of the rollercoaster when it went upside down.
    ____ b. Speed and inertia kept the cars and riders moving forward along the track.

Label each statement from the passage **F (fact)** or **O (opinion)**.
____ 12. It is the most thrilling rollercoaster in the world.
____ 13. Inertia and speed keep riders in their seats.
____ 14. Being upside down on The Corkscrew is a great feeling.

Name _____

Fourth Grade Book of Language Tests

- Three friends went on a safari to see animals.
- One person saw some elephants.
- One person saw some giraffes.
- One person saw some lions and giraffes.
- 2 of the 3 friends took pictures of the animals they saw.
- The person who saw elephants had no camera.
- Rufus Rat saw no elephants.
- Rhoda Rat saw no giraffes.
- Gigi Rat took pictures of two kinds of animals.

Read the statements about the safari.
Put an **X** by the statements that could be true, based on the information you read.

____ 15. Rufus took pictures of giraffes.

____ 16. Rhoda took no pictures.

____ 17. Rhoda took pictures of elephants.

____ 18. Gigi saw lions and giraffes.

The brave knight, Sir Reginald, was happy to have a good sword. He had slain many dragons before with his special, heavy sword. Before he had the sword made, his luck with dragons was not as good. One day, Reginald was called to protect his village from a fierce dragon. He went out to face the dragon, pulled his sword, and was shocked! Instead of his good sword, he had brought his wife's broom.

19. What will Sir Reginald probably do next?
    a. He'll battle the dragon with his wife's broom.
    b. He will run away and disappear forever.
    c. He will fight the dragon with his bare hands.
    d. He will try to get back home to get his sword.

Inferential & Evaluative Comprehension

THE SCUBA SHOP
Open more hours!
The Best Service in Town!
SCUBA GEAR AT GREAT PRICES
Everything in the store is on sale all the time.

SALES   RENTALS
All ages, All sizes
- Wet suits
- Masks
- Guages
- Fins
- Tanks
- Life Vests
- Gloves
- Cameras
- Snorkels

Broadway & Main
Open Sun-Wed, Fri-Sat, 7 am-9 pm
Call 440-1990
On the Web@ www.scubashop.com

UNDERWATER, inc
Scuba & Snorkel Gear for Kids & Teens
The Best Selection in Town
LESSONS AVAILABLE
25% off all underwater cameras
50% off all wet suits
The Best Place to Shop!
Rent a Glass-Bottom Boat

255 East Ocean Blvd
Open Mon-Sat, noon to 10 pm
Phone: 440-1111
Fax: 714-440-1234
Website: www.dive.com

20. Based on the information in the ads, which statements seem to be true? *(Circle all answers that seem to be true.)*
    a. You can sign up for lessons at either store.
    b. Children can find scuba gear at either store.
    c. **The Scuba Shop** has a good selection of scuba items for all ages.
    d. Between the two stores, a teenager could probably find what she needs.

21. Based on the information in the ads, which statements seem to be true? *(Circle all answers that seem to be true.)*
    a. You could get a good price on a wet suit at either store.
    b. You can shop for scuba gear all day any day of the week.
    c. To rent equipment, it would be best to visit **The Scuba Shop**.
    d. Both stores carry diving supplies for children.

22. What evidence is there for **The Scuba Shop's** claim that they have the best service in town?
    a. The store is open more hours.
    b. The store sells supplies for all ages.
    c. The store sells and rents equipment.
    d. All of the above reasons (a, b, and c).

23. What evidence is there for **Underwater, Inc.'s** claim that it has the best selection?
    a. The store has the lowest prices.
    b. The store rents boats.
    c. They sell more items than **The Scuba Shop**.
    d. There is no evidence for this claim.

Read this passage.

> A reporter watched the Crash County Rodeo for three hours. She noticed that the winners of all the events were wearing red bandanas. She called in to her newspaper office. She told her editor about the red bandanas. The editor wrote a story for the paper, saying that a red bandana is what caused each of these rodeo riders to win.

24. Based on the passage, what should the editor have asked before making the decision that the red bandana helped the riders win?
    a. He should have asked the names of the winners.
    b. He should have asked what events the riders won.
    c. He should have asked if the losers were also wearing red bandanas.
    d. He should have asked the ages of the winners and losers.

Use the information on this chart to answer the questions below.

Running Speed of Some Animals

Animal	Speed	Animal	Speed
Antelope	61 mph	House Cat	30 mph
Black Mamba Snake	20 mph	Lion	50 mph
Cheetah	70 mph	Quarter Horse	47.5 mph
Chicken	9 mph	Rabbit	35 mph
Coyote	43 mph	Rat	12 mph
Elephant	25 mph	Squirrel	12 mph
Fox	42 mph	Snail	0.03 mph
Giant Tortoise	0.17 mph	Spider	1.17 mph
Giraffe	32 mph	Wild Turkey	15 mph
Grizzly Bear	30 mph	Zebra	40 mph

25. Could you conclude that large animals run faster than small ones?
    _____

26. Is it likely that a chicken could outrun a spider?
    _____

27. If a zebra, coyote, and fox race, who would probably be the winner?
    _____

28. Which animals can run at least twice as fast as an elephant?
    _____

29. Which animals are slower than a spider? _____

30. Which of these animals are faster than the rat? *(Circle all that are.)*
    snake   squirrel   cat
    tortoise   chicken   rabbit

Name _____

LITERATURE SKILLS

Name _____ Possible Correct Answers: 45

Date _____ Your Correct Answers: _____

East Curryville News July 10

LOCAL CLIMBER SUES OVER PUDDING

An unusual case began today in the Curryville County Courthouse. Mountain climber, Alvira Rodent, brought a lawsuit against the Sierra Backpack Food Company. Miss Rodent testified this morning before Curry County Judge Will D. Side to explain her complaint. She claimed that the food company labeled its dried food incorrectly, and that this caused danger to her on a climbing trip. She had bought several food packages labeled *Beefy Stew* to give her strength for a difficult trip. She was counting on this as her main supply of hearty, nutritious food. But when she opened the food and added water according to directions, the food was not stew. Instead it turned into bubble gum-flavored pudding. "I needed good nutrition for a hard climbing trip," explained Alvira. "Instead, I was out in the wilderness with a pack full of junk food."

Judge Side reviewed the evidence and decided that the food company should pay Miss Rodent back for the cost of the food. In addition, he ordered the company to pay a sum of $2000 to Miss Rodent for the danger and inconvenience she experienced.

1. What is the form of this piece of writing?
   a. Imaginative story   e. Poem
   b. Essay   f. Tall tale
   c. Advertisement   g. Myth
   d. News Article   h. Fable

2. Who is the main character in this passage?
   _____

3. Who is the supporting character?
   _____

4. What is the setting of this passage?
   _____
   _____

5. From this passage, what can you tell about Miss Rodent?
   a. She is stubborn.
   b. She is serious about her health.
   c. She is a complainer.
   d. She is untruthful.

6. Which sentence is the best summary for the passage?
   a. Miss Rodent got pudding in her food packages.
   b. The Sierra Backpack Food Company put wrong labels on its food.
   c. Miss Rodent won a lawsuit against a food company for mislabeling its product.

HOW TO TELL CHICKEN POX

If you have not been camping on a hot summer night,
The little bumps all over your body are not mosquito bites.
They are chicken pox just waiting to wrap itchy fingers around you.
First, a few spots like little red paint specks will dot your cheeks.
Then they will start to grow and drip.
Next, starts the itching--
The annoying, unstopping, creeping, growing itching.
Soon, your body will look like a road map,
And the itch is forever and everywhere—even between your toes.
You might think you've got a temporary case of poison ivy.
DO NOT BE FOOLED!
Take to the nearest bathtub with a box of baking soda
And wrap bandages around your fingernails.
Afterwards, if you have scars and scabs in unusual places,
And your body has more dents than a waffle iron,
And your face looks like a polka dotted tie,
You can assume that chicken pox has gone through your life
And left you alive, but marked forever.

7. The form of this piece is _____ .

8. The theme of the piece is _____
   _____
   _____

9. The mood of the piece is:
   a. angry   d. serious
   b. fearful   e. fun
   c. joyful   f. sad

10. Write a simile or metaphor the writer uses to describe how your body looks.
    _____

11. Write four different words the writer uses to describe the itching.
    _____
    _____
    _____
    _____

12. The phrase **chicken pox just waiting to wrap itchy fingers around you** is an example of:
    a. a simile
    b. a metaphor
    c. exaggeration
    d. a pun
    e. personification
    f. rhythm

Literature Skills

HAVE A LITTLE SYMPATHY

How would you like to be stepped on five hundred times each day? Could you stand being stuffed, squashed, smashed, and squished into shoes and tied up tight for hours at a time? How would you like to be kicked against walls and balls, or forced to stomp around halls and malls? What mood would you be in if you were turned and twisted and bumped and banged day after day? And could you ever relax slanted all day in a high-heeled shoe, or painfully standing on your end wrapped in a ballet slipper? Or, how would you feel about being shoved into hot bath water, smothered in sweaty socks, or crammed without your permission into stiff, cold hockey skates? "Not at all!" you say? Well, that's what happens to feet each day.

13. Find a phrase in which the writer uses alliteration to add interest to the writing.
   _____
   _____
   _____
   _____

14. Write two phrases in which the writer uses rhyme to add interest to the writing.
   _____
   _____
   _____
   _____

15. What words does the writer use to tell about the feeling of being in socks?
   _____
   _____

16. Write 4 words or phrases that the writer uses to describe the cramped experiences of feet.
   _____
   _____
   _____
   _____

17. What is the writer's purpose in writing this piece?
   a. to explain how feet work
   b. to help readers think about what it must be like to be a foot
   c. to convince readers to stop wearing tight shoes
   d. to suggest a ban on ballet shoes

The lines and sentences below use the literary devices shown on Caspian's list. These are different ways that writers use to make writing interesting for the readers. They also help writers share with readers the ideas and feelings they want to express.

Identify one device used for each example. Write the name of the device on the line beside that example.

Alliteration
Exaggeration
Idiom
Metaphor
Personification
Repetition
Rhyme
Rhythm
Simile

_____ 18. Hippity, hippity, hop

_____ 19. Your closet is like a black hole.

_____ 20. My brother is a little steam roller.

_____ 21. You're as annoying as the hiccups!

_____ 22. My friend Rhoda is a walking calculator.

_____ 23. "Oh mercy!" said the dentist, "Oh mercy!"

_____ 24. The sun reached out and painted my body red.

_____ 25. Seven slinky slippery snakes slid silently south.

_____ 26. You're in the doghouse for forgetting your homework.

_____ 27. Hickory, Dickory, Dock, the mouse ran up the clock!

_____ 28. The kite tumbled—dipping and dropping, slipping and plopping.

_____ 29. Silently, slowly, slowly, steadily, we followed the huge footsteps.

_____ 30. It was so cold that my words froze before they reached her ears.

Name _____

Literature Skills

Once, I didn't mean to...but that was that!
I stepped in the bathtub and sat on a rat.
I'd rather take a shower with a lion or a goat,
I'd rather take a dive into a shark-infested moat,
Than slide beneath the bubbles to shampoo my hair
And latch onto the tail of a rodent swimming there.
It felt a little squishy.
It didn't bite a bit.
I bathed last night with a slippery rat
And that—was it!

31. What is the form of this piece of literature?
   _____

32. What is the setting of this piece of literature?
   _____

33. Name two main or supporting characters.
   _____
   _____

34. What is the mood of the piece?
   a. argumentative
   b. angry
   c. playful
   d. serious

35. How does the writer feel about rodents?
   a. The writer doesn't care for them at all.
   b. The writer shows no feelings about rodents.
   c. The writer had good feelings about rodents.
   d. The writer prefers cats to rats.

36. What purpose did the writer probably have in mind when writing this?
   a. to warn the reader about rats in the bathtub
   b. to convince the reader that rats are dangerous
   c. to give the reader some facts about rodents
   d. to amuse the reader

37. How did the writer feel about bathing with a rat?
   a. The writer realized it wasn't that big of a deal.
   b. The writer is totally disgusted and miserable.
   c. The writer thought it was great fun.
   d. The writer does not show any feelings about this.

Elmo's list has the names of different forms of literature.
Use one of the forms to answer each question. Write the name of the form on the line.
(A form may be used more than once.)

38. Name a form that would probably try to explain how to do something.
_____

39. Name a form that is likely to have more facts than opinions.
_____

40. Which form would probably teach a lesson?
_____

41. Which form would include stories or ideas that are great exaggerations?
_____

42. Name a form whose purpose probably would be to try to convince you of something.
_____

43. Elmo is reading a piece that tells a strange tale about a summer school in the future. The form of this is probably a (an): _____.

44. When Elmo writes an explanation to his friends about how to avoid rat traps, the form of the piece is probably a (an): _____.

45. Elmo has written a piece of literature that has lines with rhythm and rhyme.
_____

poem
imaginative story
essay
fable
news report
tall tale
recipe
advertisement
joke
MYTH
argument

Writing Skills Ckecklists

Writing Test # 1:

WORD CHOICE & WORD USE

Test Location: pages 38–39

Skill *Test Items*

Recognize and choose effective words for accurate meaning and interest 1–3
Recognize and choose precise words for strengthening written pieces 4–6
Recognize and choose active rather than inactive words and phrases 7–8
Identify words that help to create certain moods 9–10
Identify sentences which have words
    arranged in a manner that makes meaning clear 11–12
Recognize and choose words and phrases
    that produce strong visual images 13–17
Identify words or phrases that are
    repetitive or unnecessary in a written passage 18–20

Writing Test # 2:

FORMS & TECHNIQUES

Test Location: pages 40–43

Skill *Test Items*

Distinguish among the purposes of different writing forms 1–5
Identify different writing forms;
    distinguish among different writing forms 6–12
Recognize writing where form, style, or content
    fits a certain purpose for the writing 13–14
Recognize writing where form, style, or content
    appeals to a specific audience 15
Recognize sensory appeal in passages; identify examples
    that appeal to particular senses 16–18
Identify good use of details to support and enhance an idea 19
Recognize passages in which varied sentence structure and length
    makes the writing interesting and effective 20
Distinguish among different literary devices used to make writing effective 21–25
Identify examples and uses of personification 21
Identify examples and uses of exaggeration (hyperbole) 22
Identify uses of similes and metaphors 23
Identify examples and uses of idioms and puns 24
Identify examples of alliteration 25

Writing Test # 3:

CONTENT & ORGANIZATION

Test Location: pages 44–47

Skill	Test Items
Choose and use effective words in writing tasks	Task # 1
Create sentences that are clear and interesting	Task # 2
Put sentences in sensible sequence that makes meaning clear	Task # 3
Write clear questions to gain information	Task # 4
Create strong titles for written pieces	Task # 5
Create strong, attention-getting beginnings	Task # 6
Create strong, effective endings or conclusions	Task # 7
Include a clear main idea in a written passage	Task # 8
Show completeness and clear organization in a written piece	Task # 9
Use relevant details and examples to support a main idea	Task # 10

Writing Test # 4:

EDITING

Test Location: pages 48–51

Skill	Test Items
Recognize and replace overused or ordinary words and phrases	Task # 1
Recognize inactive verbs or sentences; replace these with more active sentences	Task # 2
Revise sentences for clarity	Task # 3
Eliminate excess or repetitive words or ideas in sentences	Task # 4
Arrange ideas or sentences in proper sequence	Task # 5
Revise a paragraph to vary sentence length and structure	Task # 6
Improve weak beginnings	Task # 7
Improve weak endings or conclusions	Task # 8
Replace weak or imprecise titles	Task # 9
Revise writing for accuracy in punctuation, capitalization, and other conventions	Task # 10

Writing Test # 5:

WRITING PROCESS

Test Location: pages 52–59

The writing process test is a test of writing performance. A scoring guide (pages 128–129) is used to enable the adult to give student writers a score of 1–5 in the areas of Content, Organization, Word Choice, Sentence Fluency, Voice, and Conventions.

Writing, Test #1

WORD CHOICE & WORD USE

Name _____ Possible Correct Answers: 20

Date _____ Your Correct Answers: _____

Choose the best word for each blank.

1. For twelve long days, we _____ our way through thick jungle to photograph rain forest plants.
   a. made
   b. walked
   c. whacked
   d. hiked

2. How _____ we were to see an 8-foot long python hanging right above our heads!
   a. interested   c. startled
   b. amused   d. disinterested

3. Crocodiles with _____ teeth opened their mouths to welcome anyone who might fall into their river.
   a. gigantic   c. large
   b. white   d. many

4. It's hard to sleep with the _____ noises that pierce the darkness of the jungle night.
   a. high   c. loud
   b. noisy   d. shrill

5. Gigantic mosquitoes _____ us on our entire jungle trip.
   a. pestered
   b. inconvenienced
   c. strained
   d. visited

6. "Getting caught in quicksand is a _____ experience," warned our guide.
   a. unpleasant   c. bothersome
   b. treacherous   d. pesky

7. Which sentence uses an active verb?
   a. A violent rainstorm drenched the forest.
   b. The rain is worse than yesterday.
   c. Wasn't that thunder we just heard?
   d. The air seems terribly humid today.

8. Which sentence uses an active verb?
   a. I am not happy about those crocodiles.
   b. Don't those crocodiles look menacing?
   c. Hungry jaws snapped loudly at our boat.
   d. I'm sure that crocodile is after me!

Fourth Grade Book of Language Tests   Copyright ©2000 by Incentive Publications, Inc., Nashville, TN.

9. What mood would these words and phrases help to set? _____

    muggy   steaming   dripping with sweat

    wet, heavy air   sweltering   prickly, sticky heat

10. What mood would these words and phrases help to set? _____

    hidden and puzzling   secluded

    mysteriously silent   strangely private

        hushed, whispering voices

11. Which sentence is written in a way that makes the meaning clear?
    a. Skydiving with my good friend, the pictures turned out great.
    b. The pictures turned out great while skydiving with my friend.
    c. The pictures of me skydiving with my friend turned out great.

12. Which sentence is written in a way that makes the meaning clear?
    a. Hoping to earn money for parachutes, the newspapers were delivered by the boys.
    b. Hoping to earn money for new parachutes, the boys delivered newspapers.
    c. The newspapers were delivered hoping to earn money for new parachutes.

Which sentences create **strong** visual images? *(Circle the numbers.)*

13. Rufus felt his stomach rise when the trip began.

14. Bright splashes of drifting color dotted the sky for miles.

15. There was not a sound as Rufus gently floated through the windless afternoon.

16. Shreds of the yellow balloon hung like laundry from the prickly tops of branches.

17. Clouds like fluffy piles of whipped cream wrapped around the red-striped basket that wobbled along over the green tree tops.

In each sentence, cross out any words that are not necessary.

18. The kids totally enjoyed the whole balloon ride.

19. All members of the entire group wanted to go ballooning again.

20. "Next time, we'll take a longer balloon trip when we do this again!" promised Elmo.

Name _____

Writing, Test #2

FORMS & TECHNIQUES

Name _____ Possible Correct Answers: 25

Date _____ Your Correct Answers: ____

Look at the kinds of writing that are described on Caspian's list.
Then answer the questions below.

THINGS TO READ TODAY

A an advertisement for skateboards
B a tall tale about a cat who could ride the wind
C an essay explaining how to buy a good computer
D a letter from a friend telling why you should visit
E a poster that tells all about the country of France
F a story about some friends lost in space
G instructions that come with a kite-building kit
H a news article about a blizzard
I an encyclopedia entry about ski jumping

Write one or more letters from the list to answer each question.

_____ 1. Which pieces of writing would probably try to explain something?

_____ 2. Which pieces of writing would probably try to convince you of something?

_____ 3. Which pieces of writing would probably be imaginative?

_____ 4. Which pieces of writing would probably describe the way something looks?

_____ 5. Which pieces of writing would probably include more facts than opinions?

Each sample on this page is a different form of literature. Match the forms on the list with the examples below. Write the letter of the example next to the name of the form.

___ 6. tall tale
___ 7. poem
___ 8. essay
___ 9. letter
___ 10. news report
___ 11. play
___ 12. advertisement

A. The top-selling singing group from the Stone Age will be performing at the Dell County Fair tonight. **The Smashing Boulders** will entertain audiences with old favorite hits such as The Gravel Pit Rock and Your Heart's Made of Stone. The concert begins at 7 p.m. in the Pebbles Beach Arena.

B. We were almost ready to enter our school when the ground began to rumble and shake. A huge crack opened up in the sidewalk right outside the school. To our surprise, a group of hairy cave men climbed out of the crack. They were all carrying strange instruments that looked a lot like drums and guitars. And every one of them was eating a rock sandwich.

C. The history of time travel is fascinating. For hundreds of years, brave people have been trying to find ways to visit the past or the future. Many different kinds of strange vehicles have been invented for traveling through time.

D. **Tom Shale:** Let's go down the the quarry and practice our music.
Mick Boulder: I haven't finished that new song yet.
Tom Shale: Mick! We need that finished today. The concert is in one week.

E. Dear Felix,
You probably won't believe this! I have just won a trip back into the past! All my expenses will be paid to take a time trip back to the Stone Age. Will you come along?
Your good friend,
Rufus

F. The Standing Stones, a smashing rock band
Just hired a new drummer quite grand.
Sweet Molly McMave
Who grew up in a cave,
Is now famous throughout the whole land.

G. **USED TIME MACHINES FOR RENT OR SALE**
In Good Condition
Guaranteed to Take You Somewhere You Have Never Been!
Good Prices
$1000 and up

Writing Forms & Techniques

RECIPES

Mix butter and sugar with a mixer.
Add 3 eggs, one at a time.
Beat the mixture until fluffy.
Add 2 tablespoons of vanilla.
Stir in the flour and baking powder.
Beat the mixture for 2 minutes.
Drop spoonfuls on a cookie sheet.
Smash each cookie flat with a glass.
Sprinkle with colored sugar.
Bake at 375° for 9 minutes.

Dear Santa,
Please try these cookies. I know you are on a diet. But these are very good. I made these myself, and I didn't put very much sugar into these. Please leave me a big train. I will be grateful forever.
Your best friend,
Rhodda

13. What is the purpose of this writing?
    a. to inform about something
    b. to give directions
    c. to protest something
    d. to convince someone
    e. to describe something

14. What is the purpose of this writing?
    a. to inform about something
    b. to give directions
    c. to protest something
    d. to convince someone
    e. to describe something

15. What audience do you think the writer had in mind when this was written?
    _____
    _____
    _____
    _____

KEEP YOUR KIDS HEALTHY!
Kid won't eat their vegetables?
Buy Gummy Veggie Drops!
All the vitamins & minerals kids need
Tasty, chewy fruit flavors
Buy these at your local drug store.
Try some today!

In each of these sentences, the writer is trying to appeal to a particular sense. Write the sense for each sentence.

16. The frigid wind bites my cheeks and seeps through my jacket to chill my bones. _____

17. Have you ever enjoyed such a mouth-watering, buttery batch of popcorn? _____

18. Before I entered the kitchen, my nose was teased by warm waves of cinnamon apple pie air. _____

taste
smell
touch/feeling
hearing
sight

1. Bullfighting should be banned because it is a violent sport. 2. Some fans point out how gracefully the matador moves, or how skillfully he works around the bull. 3. Other fans claim that the music and costumes make a good show. 4. They say that a bullfight is a great, exciting festival. 5. However, behind the fancy capes, loud music, and wild, cheering crowds is an awful truth. 6. Bullfights are all about blood and killing. 7. The matador and his helpers tease and anger the bull. 8. Then the helpers stick sharp sticks into the bull. 9. The bullfighter waves the cape to keep the bull charging until it gets weaker and weaker. 10. All the time, the crowd is cheering as the bull is getting nearer to death. 11. Finally the matador plunges a sword into the bull's heart. 12. This terrible routine is repeated for six bulls in each bullfight ceremony. 13. The whole tradition is cruel and horrible to watch.

19. Which sentences contain details to strengthen the idea that bullfighting is violent? (Write sentence numbers.)

_____ _____
_____ _____
_____ _____
_____ _____

20. For the passage above, which statement is true?
    a. The writer uses sentences of different kinds and lengths.
    b. All the sentences are long and complicated.
    c. All the sentences are short and choppy.

Writers use different devices to make their writing interesting.

Decide which device below is used for each example.
Write the letter code of the device on the line.

| A = alliteration | P = personification | S = simile | I = idiom | E = exaggeration |

____ 21. The fire reached out her orange fingers towards the barn.

____ 22. It was so hot that the chickens laid fried eggs.

____ 23. Your gum-chewing sounds like cows walking through mud.

____ 24. The game is cancelled because it was raining cats and dogs.

____ 25. Belinda was bothered by biting, buzzing bees.

Writing, Test #3

CONTENT & ORGANIZATION

Name _____ Possible Correct Answers: 50

Date _____ Your Correct Answers: _____

This test is made up of 10 writing tasks. Your teacher will give you a score of 1 to 5 points for each writing task, depending on how well you complete it.

TASK # 1 — WORD USE: Remember the hottest day you have ever experienced. Think about way things and people look on a very hot day. Think about the way you feel, the way the air feels, and the way things sound and smell. Think about what you'd like to eat or drink. Write a short paragraph that describes this hot day. Choose interesting, fresh, colorful words to make your readers feel the heat!

_____
_____
_____
_____
_____

TASK # 2 — CLEAR SENTENCES: Choose one of these topics. Write a clear, interesting sentence that has something to do with the topic.

some shocking news	a big explosion	a thrilling ride
a startling sound	a hilarious mistake	a spooky place
a wild dream	a big apology	an awful meal

_____
_____
_____
_____

TASK # 3 — SEQUENCE THAT MAKES SENSE: These sentences make a clear story when they are in the right order. Number them (1–7) in an order that makes sense.

____ The signs at the zoo warned people to stay behind the rail.
____ She never expected what happened next.
____ Gonzola grabbed her with one fast swipe of his big arm.
____ Susan should not have gone so close to cage.
____ Gonzola, the gorilla, seemed to motion her to come closer.
____ But Susan was fascinated by the huge, smiling gorilla.
____ She inched closer, forgetting about the box of caramel corn in her hand.

TASK # 4 — CLEAR QUESTIONS: Choose one of the people described. Assume that you want to gain information about what they have done. Write two good questions to ask the person that would help you get that information.

1. _____

a tightrope walker (at 3000 feet)
someone who's been to the moon
a submarine driver
a professional ice cream taster
a window-washer of tall skyscrapers
a 102-year-old skier

2. _____

TASK # 5 — STRONG TITLES: Write a good title or headline for each article or story. Make sure it is clearly a good label for the main idea of the written piece.

_____

Grandma Ruby Rodence called the police at dawn today. She screamed into the telephone, "My rubies are missing!" According to Grandma, she went to sleep in a locked room wearing a valuable ruby necklace. When she awoke, the door was still locked, but her jewels were missing. There are no clues or suspects.

_____

Heavy fog moved into the city this evening. Cars and trains looked like fuzzy monsters creeping through heavy, wet clouds. Yellow headlights became shiny cat's eyes appearing suddenly out of the darkness. Trees and people disappeared into a web of grey mist. Whole streets seemed to be swallowed into emptiness.

Writing Content & Organization

TASK # 6 — STRONG BEGINNINGS:
Write a strong beginning for one of these topics. Make sure your beginning will grab the attention of the reader so well that the reader will want to finish the whole piece of writing.
- a big disappointment
- a visit from someone in the past
- a tall tale about the weather
- a letter to an alien
- directions for making a milkshake
- a report of an accident

TASK # 7 — STRONG ENDINGS:
Write a strong ending for one of these topics. Make your ending memorable. Your writing should stay with the reader for a while because the ending is so fresh, unusual, surprising, or shocking.
- the blizzard of the century
- a very unusual person
- a strange discovery you made
- something you hope never happens
- a terrible day at school
- a puzzling mystery that's been solved

TASK # 8 — CLEAR MAIN IDEA: Write a short "complaint" paragraph. Explain why something makes you terribly annoyed, angry, or impatient. Make sure your paragraph makes a clear main point, so the reader understands plainly what bothers you, and why!

Name

Fourth Grade Book of Language Tests   Copyright ©2000 by Incentive Publications, Inc., Nashville, TN.

TASK # 9 — CLEAR ORGANIZATION:
TASK # 10 — GOOD DETAILS:
Write a tall tale to go along with the picture.
Make sure your tale has:
- A good title
- A strong beginning
- A strong middle
- A strong ending
- Several good details to support the main idea of the tale.

You can get a possible score of 5 points for good organization and 5 points for good details that strengthen the idea of your tall tale.

_____
(Title)

Writing, Test #4

EDITING

Name _____ Possible Correct Answers: 50

Date _____ Your Correct Answers: _____

This test is made up of 10 editing tasks. Your teacher will read your writing on each task, and will give a score of 1 to 5 points, depending on how accurately you follow the direction for each task.

Editing Task #1
REPLACE ORDINARY WORDS

Replace each ordinary word with a more colorful or interesting word. Write a new word or phrase above each crossed-out word.

A. Sirens ~~sounded~~ as the ambulance ~~drove~~ toward the crash site.

B. How long has that ~~big~~ spider been ~~going~~ across your wall?

C. What ~~good~~, ~~warm~~ pancakes!

D. It was ~~scary~~ to watch the moving tornado ~~come~~ toward our house.

E. What is this ~~weird~~ thing ~~coming~~ out of my sandwich?

Editing Task #2
REVISE INACTIVE SENTENCES:
Rewrite each sentence to make it more active.

a. Rufus went over the waterfall in a barrel.

_____
_____
_____

b. The sound of the waterfall was louder than the screaming crowd.

_____
_____
_____

Editing Task #3 — CLARIFY SENTENCES:
Rewrite the following sentences to make the meaning clear.

a. Did you read about the rat who went over Niagara Falls in that magazine?

_____
_____

b. Rufus ate a salami sandwich visiting with friends.

_____
_____

Editing

Editing Task #4 — ELIMINATE EXCESS WORDS:

Cross out the words that are repetitive or otherwise not needed.

a. The time machine looked like unicycle with one wheel.

b. A trio of three time travelers began the trip at 12 p.m. noon.

c. They packed an abundant large supply of clothing.

d. In addition, the travelers also took food and clocks.

e. The travelers said they were not at all nervous a bit.

f. It is a true fact that they really did travel through time.

Editing Task #5 — IMPROVE SEQUENCE:

These limericks do not make sense, because the ideas are not in the right order.
Number the lines in each limerick so that the sequence creates a poem that makes sense.

A. ___A spunky young fellow named Pete
    ___Till he hit the first wave.
    ___Decided to ski on his feet.
    ___Then he learned how to ski on his seat.
    ___He felt really brave,

B. ___Now she's all tangled up in a tree!
    ___Sky diver Missy McGee
    ___Not watching where she floated.
    ___Yelled, "Watch how I fall---I'm so free!"
    ___She bragged and she gloated

C. ___That the right speed for crossing is *SLOW*.
    ___Cross only on those wires that are *LOW!*
    ___Every high wire walker should know
    ___Another good rule
    ___(Unless you're a fool)—

Editing

Editing Task #6 — IMPROVE SENTENCE FLOW:
Rewrite this paragraph to make sentences that have more of a variety in length and structure. Write a paragraph that will sound smooth when it is read out loud.

How brave Caspian looked! He was going to tame a lion. He stepped into the ring. He shivered from head to toe. His arms seemed stuck to his sides. He could not even raise up the chair that would protect him. Then the cage door opened. In stepped the lion. The lion's mouth opened. Out came a fierce, terrifying roar. Caspian fainted.

_____
_____
_____
_____
_____
_____
_____
_____

Editing Task # 7 — STRENGTHEN BEGINNINGS:
Revise each of these beginnings to make them more attention-getting for a reader.

   a. The friends were floating down the river on a jungle cruise.
_____
_____

   b. It was an ordinary day at the beginning of the school year.
_____
_____

Editing Task #8 — STRENGTHEN ENDINGS:
Revise each of these endings to make them more effective and memorable.

   a. And that is the end of the tale about the disappearing teacher.
_____
_____

   b. Aren't you glad I told you this story?
_____
_____

Name _____

Editing Task #9 — STRENGTHEN TITLES:
Replace each title with a title that is more accurate and more interesting.

_____
(New title)
SCHOOL CLOSING

All schools were suddenly closed. Children were sent home. Workers left work. Roads were blocked and bridges were closed. The hurricane was coming faster than expected. Winds were blowing trees down and tearing roofs off city buildings. No one left in town could escape the storm now. It was too late.

_____
(New title)
THE CLOTHES IN THE TRAIN STATION

Who would believe that I saw an invisible person? You probably wouldn't! But I did. I saw shoes with no feet cross the street. Above the shoes, there was a coat with no legs or hands, and a hat in the air with no head. All this clothing ran into the station and caught the 8:15 train.

Editing Task #10 — CORRECT CONVENTIONS:
Fix the spelling, punctuation, capitalization, and grammar in this letter.
Cross out the errors and write the corrections above each line.

monday may 15

dear Lucy,

did you hear what is happening! Ever since sunday, parts of sandwiches have been showing up, in odd places. A pickle and some onion slices were on my porch. a pile of sliced ham was on the stairs to the bedroom. tomato chunks hung from my shower rod today? salami was in my sugar Bowl this Morning and I found swiss Cheese in my slippers. What do you think

your friend

reggie rat

Writing, Test #5   page 1 of 8

WRITING PROCESS

Name _____ Possible Correct Answers: 30

Date _____ Your Correct Answers: _____

STEP 1

The purpose of this test is to find out how you use the writing process. Read about the scoring of your paper. Then go on to the next page.

Your writing will be scored on these six traits.
You can receive 1 to 5 points on each trait.
A good piece of writing scores at least 3 points on each trait.

TRAITS

CONTENT:
The writing is clear and interesting and fun to read. It is easy for the reader to understand the main point of the paper. You have used many details that grab the attention of the reader. You give information about your topic and clearly show what is happening.

WORD CHOICE:
The words are fresh and interesting. You have avoided ordinary words. Your paper uses active verbs. You have used words and phrases that your reader will remember. The words strengthen your ideas and give them a good flavor.

VOICE:
The paper has your personal mark on it. It shows the feelings and personality of the writer. The reader can tell a human being wrote this paper. It talks directly to the reader and shows what you really think.

ORGANIZATION:
The paper starts with a catchy beginning. The writing builds up to the main point. You give good details in a clear order. A reader will want to keep reading your paper. You avoid using a lot of scattered ideas. Your paper has a good ending that readers will remember.

SENTENCES:
The sentences are clear and sound interesting. The sentences are different in length and structure. Your sentences do not all begin the same way. If you read your paper aloud, the sentences flow nicely together and sound smooth.

CONVENTIONS:
You have used punctuation and capitalization in the right places. Your spelling and grammar are correct. Each new idea is placed in a new paragraph.

STEP 2
CHOOSE ONE OF THE FOLLOWING WRITING TASKS

Writing Tasks (Choose One)

TASK # 1
Make up a story that begins like this:
It was the most terrifying sound we had ever heard.

TASK # 2
Think of a place that you think no one should ever visit. **Convince** your reader to stay away from there.

TASK # 3
Describe fireworks to someone who has never seen them before, and who has no idea what they are.

TASK # 4
Tell a true story about something funny or scary you remember from when you were a little kid.

TASK # 5
Explain how to make a spaghetti dinner or a blueberry pie.

STEP 3
COLLECT IDEAS

Write down words, phrases, sentences, and ideas that you might want to include in your paper. Put down everything that comes to mind! Think of fresh and unusual ideas. Collect colorful words. Use another piece of paper if you need more space.

STEP 4
ORGANIZE IDEAS

Make an outline, web, or list to organize your ideas. Decide on a main idea for each paragraph. Pull together ideas that support that idea.

STEP 5

WRITE YOUR ROUGH DRAFT

_____
(Title)

ROUGH DRAFT, continued...

STEP 6
EDIT YOUR WRITING

EDITOR'S GUIDE

CONTENT
___Does the writing make a clear main point that is easy to understand?
___Did I include examples or details that support the main point?
___Did I leave out details that don't relate to the main point?
___Does the paper show that I know something about the topic?
___Does it include fresh, interesting ideas?

ORGANIZATION
___Does it have a strong beginning that catches the reader's attention?
___Are the ideas written in an order that makes sense?
___Are the ideas that belong together grouped in the same paragraph?
___Will the reader want to keep on reading?
___Does the paper have a great, unusual ending?

WORD CHOICE
___Did I choose words that will capture the reader's imagination?
___Have I used some fresh, unusual, and colorful words or phrases?
___Have I used active verbs?
___Have I used words that make the meaning of the paper clear?

SENTENCES
___When I read the paper out loud, does it sound smooth?
___Are the sentences clear and interesting?
___Have I used different lengths of sentences?
___Have I used sentences that have different beginnings or structures?

VOICE
___Does my paper show personality?
___Does the writing show what I feel and think?
___Does the paper talk directly to the reader?

CONVENTIONS
___Have I used correct capitalization on sentences and names?
___Is my punctuation correct?
___Is my spelling correct?
___Do all my paragraphs contain sentences on the same idea?
___Are all my paragraphs indented?

STEP 7
WRITE YOUR FINAL DRAFT

_____
(Title)

FINAL DRAFT, continued...

Grammar & Usage Skills Checklists

Grammar & Usage Test # 1:

PARTS OF SPEECH

Test Location: pages 62–65

Skill	Test Items
Identify and distinguish among different parts of speech	1–17, 56–60
Recognize how a word is used in a sentence	11–14, 56–60
Identify and distinguish between common and proper nouns	15–16
Identify pronouns	17
Identify and form plural nouns from singular nouns	18–27
Identify and form singular nouns from plural nouns	28–37
Identify and write singular possessive nouns correctly	38, 40, 42, 43
Identify and write plural possessive nouns correctly	39, 41
Form different verb tenses	44–51
Choose or write the correct verb tense for the context	44–51
Form verb tenses with irregular verbs	47, 49, 50, 51
Identify and use action verbs	52–55
Recognize that one word can be different parts of speech, depending on its use	56–60

Grammar & Usage Test # 2:

SENTENCES

Test Location: pages 66–67

Skill	Test Items
Identify and distinguish among complete sentences, sentence fragments, and run-on sentences	1–6
Identify and distinguish among statements, questions, commands, and exclamations	7–10
Identify the complete subject of a sentence	11–13
Identify the complete predicate of a sentence	14–16
Identify the simple subject of a sentence	17–19
Identify the simple predicate of a sentence	20–22
Correct run-on sentences	23–24
Make a compound sentence from two simple sentences	25

Grammar & Usage Test # 3:

PUNCTUATION & CAPITALIZATION

Test Location: pages 68–71

Skill *Test Items*

Correct capitalization in a letter 1
Recognize correct capitalization for sentences,
    proper nouns, and adjectives 1–3
Recognize correct capitalization of titles 4–9
Use correct capitalization in a variety of situations 1–10
Identify and form contractions correctly 10–19
Identify correct use of commas 20
Properly use punctuation marks in a variety of situations 20–32
Use quotation marks properly in dialogue 22, 23
Make corrections in punctuation 21, 24–32
Make corrections in capitalization and punctuation in signs 24–32

Grammar & Usage Test # 4:

LANGUAGE USAGE

Test Location: pages 72–75

Skill *Test Items*

Choose the correct form of a verb for subject-verb agreement 1–8
Choose the correct pronoun for noun-pronoun agreement 9–13
Choose the correct possessive noun form for a context 14–15
Choose the correct subject or object pronoun for a context 16–22
Use negatives correctly 23
Avoid use of double subjects 25, 33
Correctly use verb phrases with *have* 29, 32
Identify correct use of *good* and *well*, *leave* and *let*,
    sit and *set*, *teach* and *learn*, *can* and *may*,
    don't and *doesn't* 24, 26, 27, 28, 30, 31, 34, 35
Distinguish between homonyms;
    choose correct one for a context 36–43
Choose or form the correct form of
    comparative and superlative adjectives and adverbs 44–50

Grammar & Usage, Test #1

PARTS OF SPEECH

Name _____ Possible Correct Answers: 60

Date _____ Your Correct Answers: _____

Identify the parts of speech in the sentences below.

Write **N** for noun,
V for verb,
AJ for adjective,

Which campers are madly itching with horrible poison oak?

____ 1. campers   ____ 2. madly   ____ 3. itching

____ 4. horrible   ____ 5. poison

Some creature always makes terrifying noises in the night!

____ 6. terrifying   ____ 7. creature   ____ 8. always

____ 9. makes   ____ 10. noises

Read this sentence. *Four tired, lost hikers wandered hopelessly through the dark woods.*

11. Which word is used as a **verb**? _____

12. Which words are used as **adjectives**? _____

13. Which word is used as an **adverb**? _____

14. Which words are used as **nouns**? _____

Read the sentence in Elmo's box and look for the nouns and pronouns.

15. Write the **common nouns** from the sentence.

_____

_____

16. Write the **proper nouns** from the sentence.

_____

_____

17. Write the **pronouns** from the sentence.

_____

_____

Saturday, raccoons ate our pizza from the Camp Lookout kitchen before Elmo had a chance to bring it to us in the cabin.

Write the **plural form** of each word:

_____ 18. watch

_____ 19. calf

_____ 20. potato

_____ 21. goose

_____ 22. surprise

_____ 23. canoe

_____ 24. backpack

_____ 25. donkey

_____ 26. fox

_____ 27. deer

Write the **singular form** of each word:

_____ 28. mice

_____ 29. friends

_____ 30. boxes

_____ 31. children

_____ 32. leaves

_____ 33. men

_____ 34. rubies

_____ 35. monkeys

_____ 36. radios

_____ 37. campfires

Parts of Speech

Write a **possessive noun phrase** (2 words) to fit each description.

38. oars belonging to a boat
39. tent belonging to two campers
40. hoots of one owl
41. teeth belonging to three bears
42. batteries for a flashlight
43. tail of one raccoon

38. _____ _____

39. _____ _____

40. _____ _____

41. _____ _____

42. _____ _____

43. _____ _____

Read the verb at the end of each sentence.
Write the correct form **(tense)** of the verb needed in the sentence.

_____ 44. Yesterday, Reggie _____ his canoe through the rapids. *(paddle)*

_____ 45. Will that owl keep _____ all night every night? *(screech)*

_____ 46. Rhoda hopes the poison ivy has _____ spreading. *(stop)*

_____ 47. The campers _____ a mile upstream last week. *(swim)*

_____ 48. Wear sunscreen because that hot sun _____ your skin! *(burn)*

_____ 49. Did Rufus _____ a whole pizza at supper last night? *(eat)*

_____ 50. Who _____ off the high dive just now? *(dive)*

_____ 51. Reggie _____ breakfast to the skunks this morning. *(feed)*

Parts of Speech

Write the **action verb** from each sentence.

_____ 52. The campers were not there when the earthquake struck.

_____ 53. Caspian is the funny counselor who told the joke.

_____ 54. A lifeguard is there every day to watch the swimmers.

_____ 55. Sandy was six when she built her first campfire.

56. **Crashed** is used as a verb in sentence _____ and as an adjective in sentence _____ .

    a. Thunder **crashed** all around us.

    b. Look at the **crashed** sailboat!

57. **Watch** is used as a verb in sentence _____ and as a noun in sentence _____ .

    a. **Watch** my great dive!

    b. Did you wear your **watch** in the water?

58. **Fall** is used as a noun in sentence _____ and as a verb in sentence _____ .

    a. I saw you take a nasty **fall** from your horse.

    b. Don't **fall** off that horse!

59. **Fast** is used as an adjective in sentence _____ and as an adverb in sentence _____ .

    a. If we run, we can get to the pool **fast**.

    b. Who is that **fast** runner?

60. **Hurried** is used as an adjective in sentence _____ and as a verb in sentence _____ .

    a. The **hurried** campers forgot to make their beds.

    b. The campers **hurried** to the dining hall for ice cream.

Name _____

Grammar & Usage, Test #2

SENTENCES

Name _____ Possible Correct Answers: 25

Date _____ Your Correct Answers: ____

Decide if each group of words is a complete sentence, a fragment, or a run-on sentence. Write **C** (for complete sentence), **F** (for sentence fragment), **R** (for run-on sentence).

____ 1. Going on a midnight hike.

____ 2. Wear good boots take a flashlight.

____ 3. Did you hear strange noises?

____ 4. Full moon shining all night.

____ 5. There was no rain I'm glad.

____ 6. What a great hike that was!

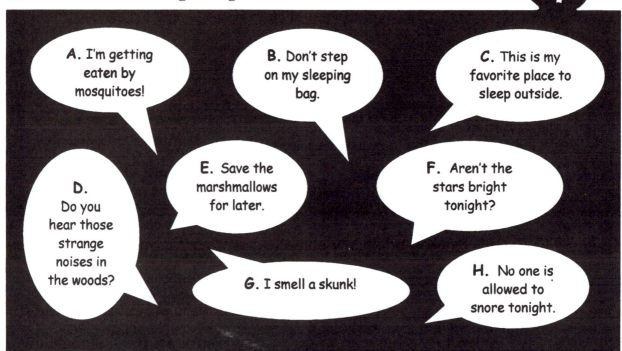

A. I'm getting eaten by mosquitoes!
B. Don't step on my sleeping bag.
C. This is my favorite place to sleep outside.
D. Do you hear those strange noises in the woods?
E. Save the marshmallows for later.
F. Aren't the stars bright tonight?
G. I smell a skunk!
H. No one is allowed to snore tonight.

Examine each quote from the campers. Decide what kind of sentence it is.

7. Which sentences are **statements**? _____

8. Which sentences are **commands**? _____

9. Which ones are **questions**? _____

10. Which ones are **exclamations**? _____

Sentences

Circle the **complete subject** in each sentence.
11. Cold, shivering campers built a fire and huddled around it.
12. Could the crackling fire get too hot?
13. The orange flames warmed our toes nicely.

Circle the **complete predicate** in each sentence.
14. We opened the bag of plump marshmallows.
15. Elmo's marshmallow fell into the fire.
16. Who burned the last batch of marshmallows?

Circle the **simple subject** in each sentence.

17. Brave campers swim in the morning.
18. The icy blue water wakes them up.
19. Many swimmers finish ten laps.

Circle the **simple predicate** in each sentence.

20. Swimmers race to the raft.
21. They love splashing each other.
22. Two of them beat the rest of us.

Correct the **run-on sentences** by writing one or more complete sentences.

23. Someone screamed, "Help!" the lifeguard ran into the water.
   _____

24. The lifeguard moved so fast she got to the swimmer in seconds.
   _____

25. Make a **compound sentence** from these two sentences. Write the new sentence on the lines below.

   A shark was spotted. The swimmers raced for safety.

   _____
   _____
   _____

Grammar & Usage, Test #3

PUNCTUATION & CAPITALIZATION

Name _____ Possible Correct Answers: 50

Date _____ Your Correct Answers: _____

1. Correct the capitalization in this letter. Write capital letters over the incorrect letters. *(10 points)*

   saturday, august 4

   dear mr. and mrs. johnson,

   greetings to you from the shores of lake lookout! your son and his cabin mates are having a great time here in wisconsin. on monday through friday, the campers swim, hike, and practice boating, sailing, and archery. our french cook makes great meals. today, they had grilled swiss cheese sandwiches. last monday, the kids watched a good movie about camping in australia and heard some unusual english ghost stories. everyone is having fun.

   sincerely,
   counselor caspian cat

   I run a happy camp.

2. Circle the words in the sentence that should have capital letters.

   camps all over the united states, from the atlantic ocean to the pacific ocean welcome campers every year from june through august.

3. Which example has the correct capitalization for this sentence?
   a. gigi learned about camp Lookout in a magazine called *Favorite Camps of america*.
   b. Gigi learned about Camp Lookout in a magazine called *Favorite camps of america*.
   c. Gigi learned about Camp Lookout in a magazine called *Favorite Camps of America*.
   d. Gigi learned about Camp Lookout in a Magazine called *Favorite Camps of America*.

Circle the numbers next to titles that are correctly capitalized.
If a title is not correct, make the changes in capitalization that will make it accurate.

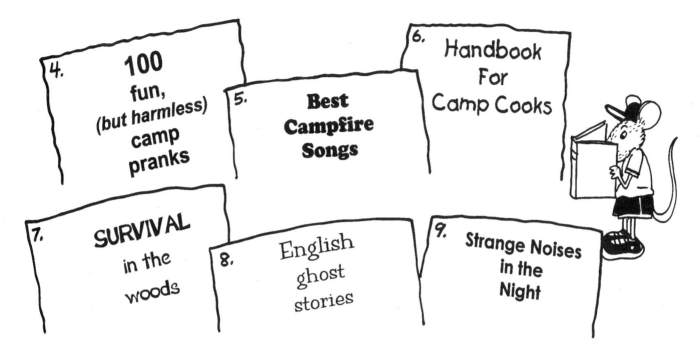

Write the two words that form the contraction.

10. they'll _____
11. won't _____
12. we'd _____
13. wasn't _____
14. you've _____

Form a contraction from the two words given.

15. would not _____
16. they have _____
17. I would _____
18. you will _____
19. are not _____

20. Which example shows correct use of commas? *(Circle the letter.)*

  a. After the storm on Monday, July 7, we ate hamburgers, salad, and cookies.
  b. After the storm, on Monday July 7 we ate hamburgers, salad, and cookies.
  c. After the storm, on Monday, July 7 we ate hamburgers, salad, and cookies.
  d. After the storm on Monday, July 7, we ate hamburgers salad and cookies.

Punctuation & Capitalization

21. Which sentences in Elmo's diary have correct punctuation?
Circle the letter of all sentences that are **correctly** punctuated. *(10 points)*

Dear Diary,
A. What a great day!
B. Ive been here since Monday July 14.
C. Why didn't I come here last year!
D. Tomorrow night, we're going on a moonlight hike.
E. Today we did three things: sailing, archery, and swimming.
F. During dinner the raccoons stole all the watches.
G. Elmo Rodney and Jake fed the raccoons late last night.
H. Gigi's poison ivy is getting worse; she itches all the time.
I. Everybody, except Rufus, ate the tuna supreme at supper.
J. Watch out for the skunks under Cabin Ten?

22. Which example shows correct punctuation for the quote? *(Circle the letter.)*

   a. "We really saw four bears on the campout, insisted Rhoda and Emily."
   b. "We really saw four bears on the campout" insisted Rhoda and Emily.
   c. "We really saw four bears on the campout," insisted Rhoda and Emily.
   d. We really saw four bears on the campout, "insisted Rhoda and Emily."

23. Which example shows correct punctuation for the quote? *(Circle the letter.)*

   a. "All right, demanded the counselor, who put the frogs in my bed?"
   b. "All right," demanded the counselor, "who put the frogs in my bed?"
   c. "All right" demanded the counselor "who put the frogs in my bed?"
   d. All right, demanded the counselor, "who put the frogs in my bed?"

All the signs around the camp need some fixing.
They have errors in capitalization and punctuation.
Fix the errors. Change small letters to capitals.
Add punctuation where needed, or change it if it is wrong.
X out any punctuation that is not needed.

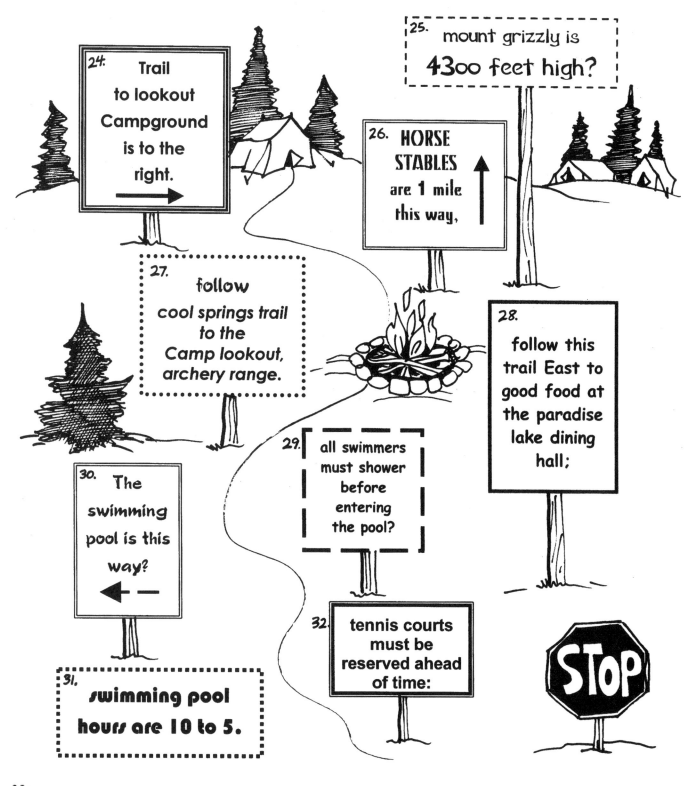

Grammar & Usage, Test #4

LANGUAGE USAGE

Name _____   Possible Correct Answers: 50

Date _____   Your Correct Answers: _____

Circle the correct form of the verb to fit in each sentence.

1. All the campers (was, were) warned about the big storm.
2. Caspian and the other counselors (have, has) been tying up the boats.
3. Rufus and I (am, are) both afraid of lightening.
4. The camp director and nurse (listen, listens) to the weather report.
5. The camp cooks (pack, packs) up some storm supplies for each cabin.
6. When the storm hits, we (snuggle, snuggles) down in our beds.
7. Thunder and lightning (crash, crashes) all around us.
8. Rufus and Reggie (hide, hides) under their covers.

Choose the correct pronouns to fit each sentences.

9. Our friends want us to share (his, their) flashlights during the storm.
10. Gigi and Sam invited us to join (him, them) for hot chocolate.
11. Sam finished his popcorn before Gigi finished (theirs, hers).
12. When we ate the popcorn, Caspian asked how we liked (it, them).
13. Every girl took popcorn back to the cabin in (her, their) backpack.

14. Which is the correct use of the possessive noun?
    a. We escaped that skunks' spray.
    b. We escaped that skunks's spray.
    c. We escaped that skunk's spray.

15. Which is the correct use of the possessive noun?
    a. Three campers' packs were lost.
    b. Three camper's packs were lost.
    c. Three campers pack's were lost.

Choose the correct pronoun for each blank.
Write the pronoun in the blank.

16. Let's go with _____ on the raft trip. (them, they)

17. Rufus has an extra raft for Gigi and _____ to use. (I, me)

18. _____ girls have experience with whitewater rafting. (Us, We)

19. Counselor Cassy said that _____ and I wear the same size wet suit. (she, her)

20. My friends and _____ looked forward to an exciting trip down the river. (I, me)

21. Which is correct?
    a. Who'll share the raft with her and I?
    b. Who'll share the raft with me and she?
    c. Who'll share the raft with she and I?
    d. Who'll share the raft with me and her?

22. Which is correct?
    a. He and I got dumped into the river.
    b. Him and I got dumped into the river.
    c. Him and me got dumped into the river.
    d. Me and he got dumped into the river.

23. Circle the letters of the sentences that use negatives **correctly**.

A. Aren't you never coming along to search for bear tracks?
B. Wouldn't you ever like to see a bear?
C. Haven't you taken any pictures yet?
D. So far I have not been able to get any pictures.
E. We have nothing to do but keep looking for tracks.
F. No one wouldn't want to miss a chance to photograph a bear.
G. That isn't like any bear I've ever seen!
H. We don't never want to go looking for bears again.

Language Usage

Every notice on the camp bulletin board has an error in the way it uses language. Find the error and cross it out or replace it with the right word.

24. I can learn anyone how to paddle a canoe.

25. The cook he wants to invite you all to a special dinner Sunday.

26. Don't sit your swim goggles down in the sand.

27. The cook says he don't need any help with breakfast tomorrow.

28. It is well to sign up for swimming lessons.

29. All campers should of registered by now.

30. Don't set too close to the edge of the cliff.

31. The counselors will leave all campers sleep in on Saturday morning.

32. We could of won the race if it had not been for the storm.

33. The birthday party it is scheduled for 9:00 p.m.

34. Let the wildflowers alone, please!

35. Didn't Cabin Ten sing good at the campfire last night?

Circle the word that correctly completes the sentence.

36. The cooks were disappointed that we did not like (there, their) meatloaf and gravy.

37. By the way, why haven't you eaten the strange-looking things on (you're, your) plate?

38. "(They're, There) is no room in my stomach for any more food," said Elmo.

39. Actually, the food has just lost (its, it's) appeal to me tonight.

40. Yes, I see that you've left your (hole, whole) dinner untouched!

41. Why don't you at least eat the (meet, meat)?

42. I (would, wood) if I could tell which thing is the meat!

43. Next time, we'll hide the bad food in (are, our) backpacks!

Read the adjective or adverb shown at the end of each sentence.
Write the correct form of that word to fit into the sentence.

44. The campers in Cabin Four were _____ than any other group. (noisy)

45. Whose ghost story was the _____ of all? (scary)

46. This is the _____ we have ever stayed awake. (late)

47. Who is _____ than Rufus tonight? (hungry)

48. One camper gets a stomachache _____ than any other. (often)

Choose the right adjective form from the end of the sentence.
Write it in the blank.

49. This is the _____ camp I've ever attended!
(good, better, best)

50. I've certainly been to several that are much _____ .
(bad, worse, worst)

Words & Vocabulary Skills Checklists

Words & Vocabulary Test # 1:

WORD PARTS

Test Location: pages 78–79

Skill	Test Items
Identify the meanings of common prefixes	1–9
Recognize and use prefixes to determine word meaning	10–22
Identify the meanings of common suffixes	23–32
Recognize and use suffixes to determine word meaning	23–32
Identify the meanings of common roots	33–42
Recognize and use roots to determine meanings of words	33–42
Recognize compound words	43–45

Words & Vocabulary Test # 2:

VOCABULARY WORD MEANINGS

Test Location: pages 80–83

Skill	Test Items
Show understanding of word meaning by answering questions about word use	1–4
Recognize meanings and definitions of words	5–10
Recognize and use synonyms	11–16
Recognize and use antonyms	17–22
Use context clues to determine a word's meaning	23–26
Choose the correct word for a particular context	27–30
Identify words with similar meanings	31–37
Identify and define words with multiple meanings	38–40

Words & Vocabulary Test # 3:

CONFUSING WORDS

Test Location: pages 84–87

Skill	Test Items
Distinguish between homonyms; select the correct one for a context	1–16
Identify and use homonyms	9–16
Distinguish between words that have similar sounds or spellings	17–23
Distinguish between words whose meanings are frequently confused with one another	24–28
Classify words according to meaning or use	29–33
Recognize the history or origin of words; recognize the meanings of words borrowed from foreign languages	34–40
Recognize the implied meanings of common idioms and other figures of speech	41–50
Use understanding of word meanings to complete analogies	51–55

Words & Vocabulary, Test #1

WORD PARTS

Name _____   Possible Correct Answers: 45

Date _____   Your Correct Answers: _____

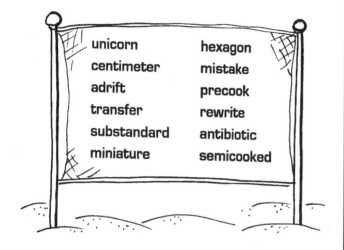

unicorn   hexagon
centimeter   mistake
adrift   precook
transfer   rewrite
substandard   antibiotic
miniature   semicooked

Write the word from the poster that has a prefix meaning.

1. against _____

2. half _____

3. wrong _____

4. before _____

5. hundred _____

6. across _____

7. small _____

8. again _____

9. below _____

Add a prefix to form a word that fits the meaning.

10. _____ view (see before)

11. _____ read (read again)

12. _____ approve (not approve)

13. _____ van (small van)

14. _____ cycle (two circles)

15. _____ port (carry across)

16. _____ human (above human)

17. _____ day (middle of day)

18. _____ stop (without stopping)

19. _____ marine (beneath the water)

20. _____ patient (not patient)

21. _____ circle (half a circle)

22. _____ place (place wrong)

Word Parts

Choose a suffix from the clouds to make a word that matches each meaning.

23. sol _____ (related to the sun)

24. wonder _____ (full of wonder)

25. pig _____ (little pigs)

26. paint _____ (one who paints)

27. window_____ (without windows)

28. wood _____ (made of wood)

29. back _____ (towards the back)

30. friend _____ (like a friend)

31. danger _____ (full of danger)

32. sail _____ (one who sails)

Look at the words on the list.

Think about the root of each word.

Write its letter next to the correct meaning of its root.

33. _____ book
34. _____ circle
35. _____ earth
36. _____ moon
37. _____ write
38. _____ work
39. _____ move
40. _____ burn
41. _____ carry
42. _____ water

A. lunar
B. geography
C. mobile
D. bicycle
E. autograph
F. flammable
G. laboratory
H. transport
I. library
J. aqueduct

Circle the compound words in each group.

43.	44.	45.
campfire	sunshine	seaweed
submarine	seasick	sailboat
camping	starfish	transport
seaside	surfing	shipwreck
surfboard	sunstroke	dangerous
telescope	sunny	underwater

Words & Vocabulary, Test #2

VOCABULARY WORD MEANINGS

Name _____   Possible Correct Answers: 40

Date _____   Your Correct Answers: _____

Circle the best answer.

1. Which would you find in the **ocean**?
   an eclipse   a casserole
   a bannister   a buoy

2. Where would you probably find a **mariner**?
   in an orchestra   at the dentist
   on a ship   in a salad

3. Where would you find a **leotard**?
   on a dancer   in a tide pool
   on a sandwich   in a church

4. What would you do with an **almanac**?
   bury it   wear it
   find facts in it put it in the bank

Choose a word from the art that matches each definition below. Write the word.

_____ 5. clap
_____ 6. foe
_____ 7. robber
_____ 8. yearly
_____ 9. punish
_____ 10. brave

80

Fourth Grade Book of Language Tests   Copyright ©2000 by Incentive Publications, Inc., Nashville, TN.

Circle the best answer.

11. Which word is a synonym for **prior**?
    important   later   previous   immediate

12. Which word is a synonym for **bizarre**?
    fair   weird   guilty   expensive

13. Which word is a synonym for **hasten**?
    chasten   crawl   decrease   hurry

14. Which word is a synonym for **punctual**?
    prompt   sharp   tardy   irregular

15. Which word is a synonym for **boast**?
    explain   complain   boost   brag

16. Which word is a synonym for **ludicrous**?
    sensible   ridiculous   tragic   inexpensive

Search the treasure chest to find an antonym for each word below.
Write the word on the line.

_____ 17. novice

_____ 18. perish

_____ 19. automatic

_____ 20. occupied

_____ 21. hearty

_____ 22. compliment

| Vocabulary Word Meanings |

Use the **context** of the sentence to decide what the **bold word** means.
(Circle the best meaning.)

23. For safety, it is absolutely **crucial** that each non-swimmer wears a lifejacket.

    The word **crucial** means: unnecessary   fashionable   important   suggested

24. Stop rocking the boat; it could tip over and **imperil** all of the boaters.

    The word **imperil** means: surprise   endanger   amuse   shock

25. Your parents did not want you to take this trip, so how were you able to come without their **consent**?

    The word **consent** means: approval   presence   money   help

26. Only the most **intrepid** surfers would dare to ride such a huge wave.

    The word **intrepid** means: cautious   friendly   daring   unusual

---

For 27–30, use **context clues** to choose the word that fits each sentence the best. *(Circle the word.)*

27. The lifeguard decided to _____ the rough play before anyone got hurt.

    encourage   squelch   join   begin   supervise

28. If you stay in the sun one minute longer, you'll be _____ your body!

    tanning   warming   harming   scorching

29. Crabs _____ slowly around the sunbathers.

    scattered   snapped   scampered   meandered

30. You'd be _____ if a shark ate your surfboard!

    irate   pleased   curious   satisfied

Name

Vocabulary Word Meanings

Cross out the word in each group that does NOT have a **similar** meaning to the other words.

31. **gloomy**	dismal	dreary	dazzling
32. **hinder**	hamper	continue	prevent
33. **agile**	quick	fragile	nimble
34. **accurate**	reckless	careless	slovenly
35. **lanky**	scrawny	skinny	stout
36. **isolate**	separate	combine	segregate
37. **imply**	impolite	hint	suggest

38. Read these different meanings for the same word.

   What is the word? _____
   a. twenty-five cents
   b. the last period in a football game
   c. a fourth

39. Read these different meanings for the same word.

   What is the word? _____
   a. the black center of the eye
   b. a student

40. Read these different meanings for the same word.

   What is the word? _____
   a. things lined up in order
   b. to paddle a boat with oars

Words & Vocabulary, Test #3

CONFUSING WORDS

Name _____ Possible Correct Answers: 55

Date _____ Your Correct Answers: _____

Circle the correct **homonym** to complete each sentence.

1. Oh, no! Elmo's life raft has just sprung a (leek, leak).
2. Are the sun's (raise, rays) able to get through those clouds?
3. Yes, you can get a sunburn (through, threw) the clouds today.
4. I think the seagulls just carried away your (pail, pale) and shovel!
5. That swimmer probably does not appreciate your (stairs, stares).
6. Don't leave your (close, clothes) too close to the water's edge.
7. The surfers must have plenty of (patients, patience) to wait for the best waves.
8. This is the (fourth, forth) crab I have seen stick his head out of a (hole, whole).

There is a WRONG homonym in each of the signs above. Write the correct homonym (a different spelling) to replace the wrong words. Write the correct words on the lines below.

9. _____   11. _____   13. _____   15. _____

10. _____   12. _____   14. _____   16. _____

Circle the correct word for each sentence.

17. The (weather, whether) forecast is for a powerful storm today.

18. The storm came, and tore right (through, though) the beach town.

19. I should have (assured, insured) my boat before the big storm hit!

20. How did the storm (effect, affect) your boat and your beach property?

21. The wind blew everything off the beach (accept, except) my car and my shoes.

22. Haven't you noticed that the water is (infected, invested, infested) with sharks?

23. Please listen to my (advice, advise) and keep everyone out of the ocean right now.

Choose the correct word from this sign to complete each sentence. Write the word in the blank.

24. Since Lucy loves the moonlight, she named her boat **Lady Lucy's _____ Lounge**.

25. When she was ready to sail, Lucy pulled up the boat's _____ and headed out of the harbor.

26. Since it rained only once, we had great weather for the _____ of the trip.

27. The gulls performed beautiful _____ dives, straight down into the water.

28. Reggie said, "I'll stay away from the water. I'm a _____ guy."

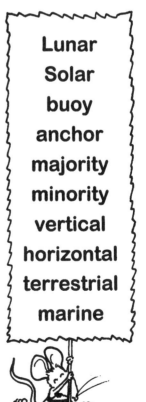

Lunar
Solar
buoy
anchor
majority
minority
vertical
horizontal
terrestrial
marine

Confusing Words

Cross out the word in each group that is NOT related to the group in the same way that the other words are related to each other.

29. seashore   shipwreck   sunshine   lifeguard   sailing

30. swimmers   lobster   rafts   babies   monkeys

31. cranky   irresistible   grumpy   irritable   touchy

32. mariner   oceanic   aquatic   sea   mare

33. wrapping   messing   memory   buttering   channelling

Below is a description of the history of some food names that are borrowed from other languages.

Write the food that matches each description. Choose from the words on the right.

_____ 34. a German word meaning **wafer**

_____ 35. a Latin word meaning **shaped like a head**

_____ 36. a Spanish word meaning **round cake**

_____ 37. a German word meaning **sour cabbage**

_____ 38. a Portuguese word for **honey**

_____ 39. a German food named after the city where it was first created: **Frankfurt, Germany**

_____ 40. a Spanish word for **round, swollen cake**

Café Menu

banana
TORTILLA
chocolate
DOUGHNUT
biscotti
SAUERKRAUT
vanilla
MOLASSES
waffle
CABBAGE
frankfurter

Write the letter of the **idiom** that matches each meaning below.

____ 41. take a risk

____ 42. very troublesome

____ 43. have second thoughts

____ 44. agree

____ 45. don't argue with me

____ 46. not very often

____ 47. say something embarrassing

____ 48. in good shape

____ 49. give away a secret

____ 50. is very expensive

SOME GOOD IDIOMS

A. *get cold feet*

B. *costs an arm and a leg*

C. *a pain in the neck*

D. *put your foot in your mouth*

E. *in mint condition*

F. *don't give me any lip*

G. *spill the beans*

H. *once in a blue moon*

I. *see eye to eye*

J. *stick your neck out*

Finish these **analogies**.

51. *Hurricane* is to _____ as *tornado* is to *land*.

52. *Porpoises* is to *porpoise* as _____ is to *mouse*.

53. _____ is to *swam* as *hurry* is to *hurried*.

54. *Frown* is to *smile* as _____ is to *dangerous*.

55. *Lifeguard* is to *beach* as _____ is to *courtroom*.

Study & Research Skills Checklists

Study & Research Test # 1:

DICTIONARY & ENCYCLOPEDIA SKILLS

Test Location: pages 90–93

Skill	Test Items
Recognize and put names in alphabetical order	1, 3, 5
Recognize and put words in alphabetical order	2
Recognize and put titles in alphabetical order	4, 7
Recognize and put phrases in alphabetical order	6
Use guide words to locate items in a dictionary	8–17
Use guide words to locate items in an encyclopedia	18–21
Identify key words for finding information in an encyclopedia	22–25
Use a dictionary to find word meanings	26–27
Use a dictionary to find information about words other than meanings	28–30
Find information in an encyclopedia entry	31–35

Study & Research Test # 2:

REFERENCE & INFORMATION SKILLS

Test Location: pages 94–99

Skill	Test Items
Identify the uses of a variety of reference materials	1–8
Select the best reference material for an information-gathering task	9–22
Identify the purposes of various parts of a book	23–27
Find and interpret information in a Table of Contents	28–34
Find and interpret information in an index	35–42
Interpret information from an illustration	43–44
Find and interpret information on a map	45–49
Find and interpret information on a timeline	50–53
Find and interpret information on charts, tables, and graphs	54–60

Study & Research Test # 3:

LIBRARY SKILLS

Test Location: pages 100–101

Skill	Test Items
Show understanding of the library system for classifying fiction	1, 4
Show understanding of the library system for classifying non-fiction	2, 3
Understand how to use a library catalog to locate books	5
Find information on library cards	6–12
Show understanding of categories of books (fiction, biography, non-fiction other than biography)	13–20

Study & Research Test # 4:

STUDY SKILLS

Test Location: pages 102–103

Skill	Test Items
Form good questions to gain information	1
Gain information quickly by skimming a passage	2–4
Identify the main idea in a passage	5
Identify ideas in a passage that support the main point	6
Summarize a passage	7
Use an outline to organize information	8–10

Study & Research Skills Test #1

DICTIONARY & ENCYCLOPEDIA SKILLS

Name _____   Possible Correct Answers: 35

Date _____   Your Correct Answers: _____

1. Number these business names 1 to 5 in the correct **alphabetical order**.

   _____ Dewey Detective Agency
   _____ Best Detectives, Inc.
   _____ Be Safe Investigations
   _____ Detecting Experts
   _____ Double Duty Detectives

2. Which of the following groups is in alphabetical order?

   a. mystery, mister, mysterious, master
   b. mister, mysterious, mystery, master
   c. master, mister, mysterious, mystery

3. Which of the following groups is in alphabetical order?

   a. Boise, Boston, Britain, Buffalo
   b. Britain, Boise, Boston, Buffalo
   c. Boise, Boston, Buffalo, Britain

4. Number these titles 1–4 in alphabetical order.

   _____ *The Case of the Stolen Jewels*
   _____ *The Case of the Missing Tacos*
   _____ *The Case of the Hungry Rat*
   _____ *The Case of the Honest Burglar*

5. Number these names 1–4 in alphabetical order.

   _____ Antarctica
   _____ Amazon River
   _____ Arctic Circle
   _____ Atlantic Ocean

6. Number these phrases 1–5 in alphabetical order.

   _____ run errands
   _____ run around
   _____ run for president
   _____ run away with
   _____ run over

7. Number these titles 1–4 in alphabetical order.

   _____ *How to Start a Detective Business*
   _____ *How to Track a Suspect*
   _____ *How to Become Invisible*
   _____ *How to Take Perfect Fingerprints*

Use the dictionary **guide words** to answer questions 8–17.

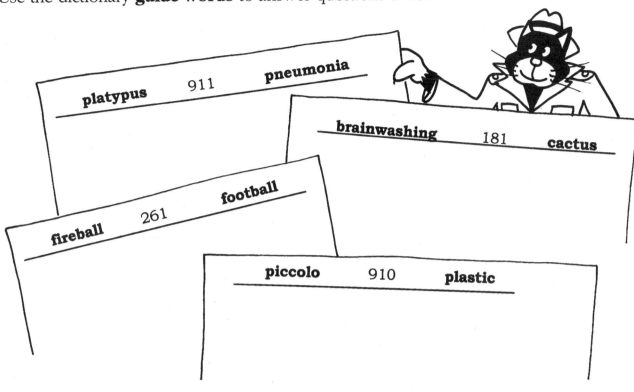

8. Would **Braille** be found on page 181? _____

9. On what page would you find **pigskin**? _____

10. Would **pledge** be found on page 911? _____

11. Would **footloose** be found on page 261? _____

12. Would **bubble gum** be found on page 181? _____

13. On what page would you find **plop**? _____

14. Would **photograph** be found on page 910? _____

15. Would **pickle** be found on page 910? _____

16. Would **bull's eye** be found on one of these pages? _____

17. Would **freeze-dry** be found on page 911? _____

Name _____

Dictionary & Encyclopedia Skills

Use the **encyclopedia guide words** to answer questions 18–21.

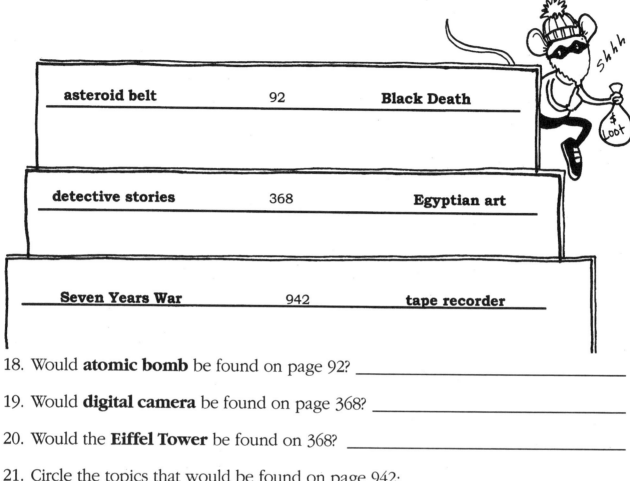

asteroid belt	92	Black Death
detective stories	368	Egyptian art
Seven Years War	942	tape recorder

18. Would **atomic bomb** be found on page 92? _____

19. Would **digital camera** be found on page 368? _____

20. Would the **Eiffel Tower** be found on 368? _____

21. Circle the topics that would be found on page 942:

    Taiwan   *Seven Wonders of the World*   *table tennis*   *Turkey*

When you look for a topic in an encyclopedia, you try to look under a **key word** that will lead you to the topic most quickly. Circle the best **key word** for each of these topics.

22. To find the number of rings around the planet Saturn you would look under:

    rings   Saturn
    planets   universe

23. To learn about products grown or produced in Kansas, you would look under:

    products   United States
    Kansas   states

24. To find the names of brass orchestra instruments, you would look under:

    brass   music
    instruments   orchestra

25. To find the name of some famous fictional detectives, you would look under:

    detectives   mystery
    fiction   stories

Name _____

Dictionary & Encyclopedia Skills

Use these dictionary entries to answer questions 26–30.

my-al-gi-a \mī 'al j(ē)ə\ *n. Pathology.*
Muscular pain. [New Latin: MYO = algia]

mys-te-ri-ous \mis 'tir ē əs\ *adj.*
1. Full of mystery; difficult to explain.
2. Beyond human understanding.
3. Strange. [Old French *muysterieux*]
—**mys-te-ri-ous-ly** *adv*
—**mys-te-ri-ous-ness** *noun*

mys-ter-y \'mis t(ə-) rē\ *n., pl* **-ies**
1. Anything that causes curiosity because it is unexplained. 2. Something secret or unknown. 3. A piece of fictional writing that deals with mystery or crime.
4. Secretive behavior. [Middle English *mysterie*, from Late Latin *misterium*.]

26. What is the meaning of **myalgia**? _____

27. Which meaning of the word **mystery** is used in the sentence below? (Write the number of the meaning.) _____
    I'm going to read a good mystery.

28. From what language does the word **myalgia** come? _____

29. How many meanings are shown for **mysterious**? _____

30. Write the plural of **mystery**.
    _____

Use this encyclopedia entry to answer questions 31–35.

Bermuda Triangle A region in the Atlantic Ocean where many strange disappearances have taken place. The Bermuda Triangle covers about 440,000 square miles between the island of Bermuda, Puerto Rico, and the coast of Florida. In 1918, a ship, the *U.S.S. Cyclops*, disappeared. Since that time, several other ships, boats, and planes have disappeared in this area, vanishing without a trace.

Some think the ships have been abducted by aliens, or pulled into a hole in the sky by some unknown force. Others think there are reasonable explanations for the strange occurrences in the Bermuda Triangle.

31. What has disappeared in the Bermuda Triangle? _____
32. How much space does the Bermuda Triangle cover? _____
33. In what ocean is the Bermuda Triangle? _____
34. When did the *U.S.S. Cyclops* disappear? _____
35. What are two of the explanations people give for the strange happenings in this area?
    _____

Study & Research Skills, Test #2

REFERENCE & INFORMATION SKILLS

Name _____ Possible Correct Answers: 60

Date _____ Your Correct Answers: _____

REFERENCES to REMEMBER

A. almanac
B. atlas
C. biographical dictionary
D. book of records
E. dictionary
F. encyclopedia
G. geographical dictionary
H. newspaper
I. telephone directory
J. timeline

Below are descriptions of different reference materials.
Match them with the names of the reference books on the detective's notepad.

Write the letter of the reference on the line before the correct description.

____ 1. an alphabetical list of places in the world and their descriptions and locations

____ 2. a list of events arranged on a diagram in order of their dates

____ 3. a collection of news, articles, features, and advertising published daily or weekly

____ 4. a book of current records of sporting events and various other events

____ 5. a collection of words arranged alphabetically, containing information about the words' meanings, uses, forms, pronunciations, and histories

____ 6. a collection of maps bound into a book

____ 7. a book that is published yearly, containing a variety of general and numerical information

____ 8. a collection of information in one or more volumes on many subjects, gathered together in articles that are alphabetically arranged

Which reference should you use to find each of the following kinds of information? Choose the best reference for each task from Detective Felix's list. Write the letter of the reference on the line.

A. atlas
B. almanac
C. biographical dictionary
D. dictionary
E. encyclopedia
F. encyclopedia index
G. geographical dictionary
H. <u>Guinness Book of Records</u>
I. Internet
J. library catalog
K. newspaper
L. thesaurus
M. telephone directory

____ 9. a weather forecast for tomorrow in Munich, Germany

____ 10. the correct pronunciation of the word **petit fours**

____ 11. a weather forecast for tomorrow in your city

____ 12. five words that mean the same as **carousel**

____ 13. information about the Abominable Snowman

____ 14. the author of the books about Harry Potter

____ 15. the titles of some poetry books by the author Shel Silverstein

____ 16. a short biography of Sandra Day O'Connor

____ 17. the location of Malaysia

____ 18. the present population of India

____ 19. which volume of an encyclopedia describes UFOs

____ 20. a synonym for the word **impetuous**

____ 21. the name of the current record holder for lawnmower racing

____ 22. a list of sporting goods stores in your area

Reference & Information Skills

Write the book part that matches each of the definitions in 23–27.

index

table of contents

cover

title page

glossary

copyright page

_____ 23. the first page of the book; contains the title, author, and publisher

_____ 24. a list of sections in the book and their page numbers, arranged in the order they occur in the book

_____ 25. a list of terms used in the book, along with their definitions

_____ 26. a page near the front of the book; contains the name of the publisher and copyright date

_____ 27. an alphabetical list of topics in the book and their page numbers; found at end of book

The Kids' Book of Disguises
Table of Contents

Kinds of Disguises	8
Ch 1: Make-Up & Makeovers	12
Using Makeup for Disguise	13
Changing the Look of Your Face	18
Ch 2: Hair Changes	30
Wigs and Other Hair Pieces	31
Beards & Mustaches	37
Ch 3: Clothing Disguises	42
Hats and Shoes	43
Coats and other Clothing	46
Ch 4: Body Changes	61
Gestures	62
Voice Changes	73
Movement Changes	80
Ch 5: Shopping for Disguises	100
Glossary	102
INDEX	106

Use the Table of Contents to answer questions 28–34.

28. On what pages can you read about using facial hair as disguises? _____

29. What chapter covers use of make-up for disguises? _____

30. Which chapter is the longest? _____

31. Which pages give a definition of disguises? _____

32. On what pages can you read about changing the way you move? _____

33. What pages explain how to disguise your voice? _____

34. How long is the glossary? _____

Name _____

Fourth Grade Book of Language Tests

Use the Index for questions 35–42.

INDEX

Beards, 37-39
Body Language, 61-99
Buying disguises, 100-101
Coats, 46-47
Clothing, 42-60
  Coats, 46-47
  Dresses, 48-50
  Hats, 43-44
  Shirts, 55-60
  Shoes, 45
  Slacks, 51-54

Footwear, 45
Gestures, 62-72
  Hand, 62-69
Hats, 43-44
Hair, 30-41
  Facial, 37-41
  Beards, 37-39
Hand gestures, 62-69
Kinds of disguises, 8-11
Looks, changing, 12-29
Make-Up, 13-17

Movement, 80-99
Mustaches, 40-41
Posture, 83-84
Shirts, 55-60
Shoes, 45
Slacks, 51-54
Shopping, 100-101
Style of movement, 80-81
Voice changes, 73-79
Walking, 88-92
Wigs, 31-36

Write the page numbers in the book on which each of these topics could be found.

35. Wigs _____

36. Facial Hair _____

37. Voice Changes _____

38. Mustaches _____

39. Hand gestures _____

40. Changing your looks _____

41. Kinds of disguises _____

42. Body Language _____

Answer these questions after studying the picture below.

43. Which of these is probably true?

    a. Rufus has hurt himself.

    b. Rufus is feeling sick.

    c. Rufus does not like cheese.

44. Which of these can you tell from the picture?

    a. It is nighttime.

    b. It is daytime.

    c. It is a stormy day.

    d. You cannot tell any of these.

Name _____

Reference & Information Skills

Use the map for questions 45–49.

45. Which road runs east and west?
_____

46. What direction is the airport from Spy Lake?
_____

47. Which town is south of Curious County Highway?
_____

48. What road goes to Snoop Village?
_____

49. Which roads cross the river?
_____

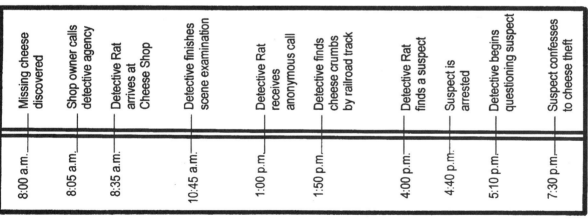

Use this timeline for questions 50–53.

50. How long after the discovery of the missing cheese was the arrest made?
_____

51. How long did it take Detective Rat to get to the crime scene?
_____

52. What happened 3 hours after the anonymous phone call?
_____

53. How long did Detective Rat question the suspect?
_____

Name _____

Fourth Grade Book of Language Tests

Use this table for questions 54–57.

Investigations of Strange Disappearances

Kind of Case (Type of Missing Things)	Det. J.B. Sharp	Det. C.C. Catcher	Det. D.D. Scover	Det. R.J. Surch
Food Items	12	1	9	12
People	2	4	4	1
Vehicles (Trains, Cars, Planes)	3	1	4	2
Pets	10	8	0	0
Jewelry	0	9	17	12

54. Which detective was busiest?

55. Which detective investigated the most jewelry cases?

56. How many missing pets cases did J.B. Sharp investigate?

57. Which kind of disappearance totaled 34 cases?

Use this graph for questions 58–60.

58. How many cases were solved in June?

59. In which month were 26 cases solved?

60. How many months were busier than February?

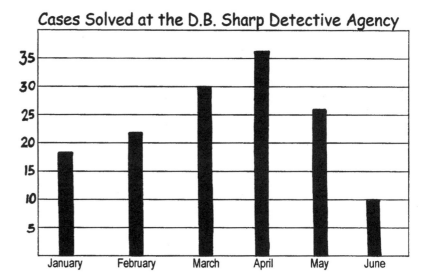

Study & Research Skills, Test #3

LIBRARY SKILLS

Name _____ Possible Correct Answers: 20

Date _____ Your Correct Answers: _____

1. In what order would these books be found in a library fiction section? *(Circle one.)*
   A-B-C   A-C-B   B-A-C   B-A-C   C-A-B   C-B-A

2. In a library, biographies are organized:
   a. alphabetically by author
   b. alphabetically by title
   c. alphabetically by subject
   d. alphabetically by publisher

3. In a library, non-fiction is organized:
   a. alphabetically by author
   b. alphabetically by title
   c. by a numbering system
   d. alphabetically by subject

4. Fiction is organized:
   a. alphabetically by author
   b. alphabetically by title
   c. by the Dewey Decimal System
   d. alphabetically by subject

5. To find a humorous book by the author Mark Twain, which word would you type into the library computer catalog?
   a. Mark   c. humor
   b. Twain   d. fiction

```
796     SPORTS-ANECDOTES
Je         Jewel, Angela
        Funniest Sports Mistakes
           Illust. by Harvey Davis
        Chicago: Erwin & Sons. © 1999
           220 p.  illus.
```

```
599.64  STANLEY, FELIX
Sta     Pythons and Boa Constrictors
           Illust. by G. Gordon Brown
        NY: Truman Publishing © 1996
           140 p.  illus.
```

6. What kind of library catalog card is this?
   a. author card
   b. subject card
   c. title card

7. Who is the publisher of this book?
   _____

8. What is the book's title?
   _____

9. What kind of library catalog card is this?
   a. author card
   b. subject card
   c. title card

10. What is the copyright date? _____

11. Who is the illustrator?
    _____

12. How many pages are in the book?
    _____

Read the titles of the books below.
Decide whether each book is probably a fiction book,
a biography, or a non-fiction book other than a biography.
Write **F** for fiction, **B** for biography, **N** for non-fiction.

_____ 13. *The Cow Who Wanted to See the Statue of Liberty*

_____ 14. *Peggy Fleming: An Olympic Ice Skater*

_____ 15. *Amazing Facts about Rats and Other Rodents*

_____ 16. *Great Math Puzzles*

_____ 17. *Learn to Speak French*

_____ 18. *The Strange Disappearance of the Gold Medal*

_____ 19. *How to Understand Your Parents*

_____ 20. *The Life Story of Scuba Diver I. C. Fish*

Study & Research Skills, Test #4

STUDY SKILLS

Name _____ Possible Correct Answers: 10

Date _____ Your Correct Answers: _____

CASE # 1
Detective C. Cat received a strange emergency phone call at 12:05 p.m. The frantic caller reported that his favorite kind of pizza was appearing on his doorstep every day at noon. At first, he enjoyed the pizzas, but now he was afraid that something sinister might be going on. Detective Cat grabbed his notebook and headed out to see if he could solve the mystery of the appearing pizzas.

CASE # 2
It was just beginning to rain when Gigi left home for a visit to the zoo, so she grabbed an umbrella. "What a nasty rain!" she heard a voice say. Gigi saw no one around, and thought she must have imagined the voice. "Well, don't you think so?" the voice asked again. Gigi saw no one. There were no more voices until Gigi reached the zoo. The rain stopped, so she closed the umbrella. "Help!" It is wet and soggy in here. Open me up to dry out!" Gigi was shocked to realize that the voice belonged to the umbrella!

1. Which of these questions should the detective use to help him solve the mystery of the pizzas? Circle the letters of the questions that would be helpful.

   a. Exactly what days has this happened?

   b. What store or restaurant makes the pizza?

   c. What is your favorite kind of pizza?

   d. Have you asked the neighbors if they've seen anyone deliver the pizza?

   e. Have you ever seen anyone deliver the pizza?

   f. What toppings are on the pizza?

   g. Who knows what kind of pizza you like?

Skim Case # 2 quickly. Without looking back through the story, answer these questions.

2. What was the first strange thing Gigi heard the voice say?
   _____

3. Where was Gigi when the voice yelled, "Help"?
   _____

4. What did the Gigi think when she first heard the voice?
   _____
   _____

Fourth Grade Book of Language Tests

CASE # 3

Rhodda was delighted with her new painting, a gift from her friend, Elmo. The painting was a very realistic scene of busy rats, happily scurrying around to sweep and clean their cozy home. She put on her green nightshirt and went to sleep in her slightly messy bedroom. Imagine her surprise when she awoke to find a spotless, perfect room! She was sure the rats had cleaned it. This happened every night. She awoke each morning to find the dishes washed, the laundry clean, and the floors swept. Her refrigerator had even been cleaned! Each morning her hands were sore with blisters. She told all her friends that the rats were cleaning her house. They suggested she hire a detective to find out what was really happening. They just could not believe that the rats had come out of the painting to clean at night!

5. What is the main idea of the story?

_____

_____

_____

6. Which details are important to an explanation of the mystery?

   a. Gigi slept in her green nightshirt.
   b. The painting was a gift.
   c. Her room was clean each morning.
   d. She told all her friends.
   e. Her room was messy at night.
   f. Her hands were sore each morning.

CASE # 4

Elmo proudly put his savings for the week in his piggy bank and went to sleep. His door was locked, assuring that his full bank would be safe. In the morning, the bank was just where he left it. But it was empty! How could this be? No one had a key to his room! Elmo was beside himself with grief.

7. Which is the best summary of Case # 4?
   a. Elmo's money disappeared overnight.
   b. Elmo saved money in his piggy bank.
   c. Elmo was sad about losing the money.

Write the numbers and letters to show where each of these missing pieces belongs in the outline below. (Example: III A)

____ 8. Custard was on the doorknob.

____ 9. Two dozen cream puffs were gone.

____ 10. Henri locked the door.

The Case of the Missing Cream Puffs
I. Henri baked 5 dozen cream puffs.
  A. He finished them at midnight on Monday.
  B.
II. Henri discovered a theft.
  A. He got to the bakery at 6 a.m. Tuesday.
  B. The doors were still locked.
  C. He looked in the refrigerator.
  D.
III. Henri looked for clues.
  A.
  B. Crumbs were on the floor.
  C. His 10-year old son, Henri Jr., had a tummy ache.

Spelling Skills Lists

Spelling Test # 1:

RULES & RULE-BREAKERS

Test Location: pages 106–107

Skill	Test Items
Skill	*Test Items*
Correctly spell words that use the *ie* rules	1–9
Correctly spell words with double consonants	10–15
Spell words with confusing initial consonant sounds and blends	16–21
Correctly spell the singular form of a plural noun	22–27
Correctly spell the plural form of a noun	28–33
Correctly spell a variety of compound words	34–36
Correctly spell the past tense of words	37–44
Correctly spell words that break spelling rules	45–50

Spelling Test # 2:

SPELLING WITH WORD PARTS

Test Location: pages 108–109

Skill	*Test Items*
Correctly spell words with prefixes	1–8
Correctly spell words with suffixes	9–16
Correctly spell words that have a prefix and a suffix	4, 5, 7
Use knowledge of root spellings to spell words correctly	17–24
Make correct changes to root words when adding *ed* or *ing*	25–30
Distinguish among similar endings; choose the correct ending for accurate spelling	31–40

Spelling Test # 3:

CONFUSING & TRICKY WORDS

Test Location: pages 110–111

Skill	Test Items
Correctly spell words that contain silent letters	1
Correctly spell words of foreign origin	2–9
Correctly spell words with special vowel combinations	10–15
Correctly spell big words	16
Correctly spell a variety of confusing words	17–26, 27–35
Spell and distinguish between words that sound alike	27–30
Spell and distinguish between words that look or sound similar	31–35

Spelling Test # 4:

CORRECTING SPELLING ERRORS

Test Location: pages 112–116

Skill	Test Items
Find spelling errors in proper nouns	1–5
Identify words that are correctly spelled	6–11, 26
Choose the correct spelling of a word	12–17
Identify words that are incorrectly spelled	18
Correct the spelling of misspelled words	19–25, 27–32
Correct misspelled words within a sentence	33–37
Use knowledge of spelling to edit signs, titles, or headlines	38–39, 41–60
Use knowledge of spelling to edit brief passages	40

Spelling, Test #1

RULES & RULE-BREAKERS

Name _____ Possible Correct Answers: 50

Date _____ Your Correct Answers: _____

Circle the correct spelling for each word.

1. grief   4. receive   7. wieght   9. ceiling
   greif   recieve   weight   cieling

2. beleive   5. piece   8. nieghbor
   believe   peice   neighbor

3. freind   6. sleigh
   friend   sliegh

nesessary   catterpillar   vacuum   drumming
embaras   tomorrow   marshmallow
scisors   comitee   bannannas   accident

Find the words on the banner that are spelled incorrectly. Write them correctly.

10. _____ 12. _____ 14. _____

11. _____ 13. _____ 15. _____

Find the misspelled word in each sentence.
Cross out the word, and write it correctly on the line by the sentence.

_____ 16. The crowd wistled as the circus began.

_____ 17. Elephants paraded in sircles.

_____ 18. Clowns did jymnastic tricks.

_____ 19. We all ate karamal corn.

_____ 20. The cotton candy was full of shugar.

_____ 21. The performance ended too kwickly.

Fourth Grade Book of Language Tests   Copyright ©2000 by Incentive Publications, Inc., Nashville, TN.

Spelling Rules & Rule-Breakers

Write each noun in its **singular** form.

22. potatoes _____
23. children _____
24. mice _____
25. cities _____
26. foxes _____
27. gorillas _____

Write the **plural** form of each noun.

28. goose _____
29. pony _____
30. scarf _____
31. donkey _____
32. echo _____
33. gentleman _____

Circle the **compound words** that are spelled correctly in each group.

34. homwork   35. houskeeper   36. seashell
    sunsset   bedspread   blubird
    dragonfly   waterrfalls   roomate
    flashlight   firworks   snoball

Write each word in its **past** tense.

37. marry _____
38. watch _____
39. go _____
40. forget _____
41. argue _____
42. bring _____
43. sing _____
44. apply _____

These words are all rule-breakers.
Circle the **correct spelling** for each pair.

45. truly   truely
46. sience   science
47. hieght   height
48. soloes   solos
49. weird   wierd
50. foriegn   foreign

Name _____

Spelling, Test #2

SPELLING WITH WORD PARTS

Name _____ Possible Correct Answers: 40

Date _____ Your Correct Answers: _____

All the words on Felix's test have prefixes or suffixes. Which words has he spelled correctly? Circle the numbers of the correctly spelled words. Fix the wrong words. Write them correctly on the lines following the words.

SPELLING TEST

1. preepare _____
2. subbmrine _____
3. immpolite _____
4. semicircular _____
5. departure _____
6. nonsence _____
7. antebiotic _____
8. transffer _____
9. argument _____
10. hopeless _____
11. friendlyness _____
12. wonderfull _____
13. quickly _____
14. dangereous _____
15. gravitty _____
16. pianoist _____

Use your knowledge of **roots** to spell these words correctly. They all have errors.

17. musicel _____
18. appeerance _____
19. laberatory _____
20. mountinous _____
21. diffrence _____
22. dentestry _____
23. misspel _____
24. disaprove _____

Add *ed* or *ing* to the word at the end of the sentence to make it fit correctly. Write the word in the blank. Make sure you spell it correctly!

25. The cousins _____ to get in line for the concert. *(hurry)*

26. They went _____ to the concert hall where they stood in line for hours in an icy wind. *(run)*

27. "We're _____ to get seats in the front row," said Rufus. *(hope)*

28. The fans have been _____ this band for years. *(praise)*

29. The loud music _____ through the whole hall. *(echo)*

30. "This _____ hurts my ears!" shouted Rhoda. *(clap)*

Some of the words below have incorrectly-spelled endings. Circle the correctly-spelled words.

31. excitemant   excitement   excitemint
32. candle   candel   candal
33. vacashun   vacation   vacaton
34. surprise   surprize   surprice
35. possable   possibel   possible
36. favirate   favirete   favorite
37. travel   travil   traval
38. chocolit   chocolet   chocolate
39. gargedge   garbidge   garbage
40. nervus   nervous   nerveous

Spelling, Test #3   page 1 of 2

CONFUSING & TRICKY WORDS

Name _____   Possible Correct Answers: 35

Date _____   Your Correct Answers: _____

1. Which words on Caspian's pillow have silent letters? Circle them.

Look at these words borrowed from other languages.
Decide if each one is spelled correctly.
If it is NOT, write it correctly on the line.

2. mosquitoe _____
3. vanilla _____
4. octapus _____
5. dimond _____
6. piano _____
7. pyjamas _____
8. tornado _____
9. umbrella _____

Which pair of vowels is right for each of these words? Choose the correct pair and write it in the blank to spell the word correctly.

10. fount _____ n   **ea   ai   ia**

11. qu _____ t   **ae   ie   ei**

12. n _____ sy   **oy   oi   ow**

13. c _____ gh   **ow   au   ou**

14. p _____ ple   **ee   eo   ea**

15. ch _____ t   **ea   ae   ee**

16. Circle the words that are **spelled correctly** on Pierre's masterpiece.

Which is the **correct spelling** for each of these words?

17. a. calender
    b. calendar
    c. calandar

18. a. favorite
    b. faverite
    c. favorate

19. a. nesessary
    b. necesary
    c. necessary

20. a. busness
    b. business
    c. bussness

21. a. lonlyness
    b. lonliness
    c. loneliness

22. a. accident
    b. axcident
    c. accadent

23. a. restrant
    b. restaurant
    c. restraunt

24. a. vegtables
    b. vegetables
    c. vegatables

25. a. memry
    b. memary
    c. memory

26. a. surprise
    b. suprize
    c. surprize

Circle the word that correctly finishes the sentence.

27. "Hurray!" they shouted (allowed, aloud) in the library.

28. I wish you had not (thrown, throne) my best hat away.

29. What are those weird bugs on my (sealing, ceiling)?

30. For a joke, I (sent, cent, scent) a pet skunk to my friend.

31. Gigi writes every day in her (dairy, diary).

32. This (caller, collar) has been trying to reach you all morning.

33. We play tennis every day (accept, except) Sunday.

34. How many (angels, angles) are in a decagon?

35. A clever cat is my favorite (cartoon, carton) character.

Spelling, Test #4

CORRECTING SPELLING ERRORS

Name _____ Possible Correct Answers: 60

Date _____ Your Correct Answers: _____

One **proper noun** in each group is spelled correctly. Circle it.

1. California, Montanna, Flordia
2. Saterday, Thursday, Wenesday
3. Jupater, Satturn, Earth
4. Miami, Bosten, Chichago
5. Cannada, Rushia, Mexico

Are these words spelled correctly? Write *yes* or *no* next to each word.

6. chorus _____
7. languge _____
8. tward _____
9. excellent _____
10. choclate _____
11. tongue _____

Circle the **correct spelling** of each word.

12. sandwich
    sammich
    sandawich
    sandwitch

13. twelth
    twelvth
    twelveth
    twelfth

14. oppisite
    oposite
    opposite
    oppasite

15. caccon
    coccoon
    caccoon
    cocoon

16. serious
    sereous
    serius
    sereous

17. enuf
    enugh
    enough
    eanough

Correcting Spelling Errors

18. Which words in the picture are spelled wrong? Write them correctly on the lines below the picture.

adventure lafter
elephent
sircus juggler
dangerous magician
trapeeze wierd
enttertain

_____

_____

_____

_____

_____

In each pair of words, ONE is misspelled. Write it correctly.

19. teriffick, absence _____

20. impossable, icicle _____

21. stomack, general _____

22. exersise, excuse _____

23. memory, realise _____

24. toungue, enough _____

25. empty, biscit _____

26. How many words in the magician's hat are spelled INCORRECTLY?

_____

supprise
secret
miracle
MAGIKAL
inquire
mistery
unbelievable
rabbitt SPECIAL

Correcting Spelling Errors

Some of the juggler's words are spelled incorrectly. Find them and write them correctly.

27. _____
28. _____
29. _____
30. _____
31. _____
32. _____

In each sentence, find a word that is misspelled. Write it correctly on the line before the sentence.

_____ 33. Lily, the brave lion tamer, had ofen faced fierce lions.

_____ 34. Tonight, instead of having courage, she was num with fear.

_____ 35. She forgot all she knew about handeling lions.

_____ 36. When the lion entered the cage, he could tell Lily was frihtened.

_____ 37. Luckily, Lily was able to make an excape out the cage door.

Correcting Spelling Errors

Some words on the circus posters are not spelled correctly.
Cross out each misspelled word. Write it correctly near the word on the poster.

38.

THE GREATEST SHOW ON THE PLANIT
DANCING ELAPHANTS
Restling Monkeys
Singing Gorrillas
Magnificent Aminal Parade
Special Shows at Noon
New York—Chicago—Dallas
Tickets: $15

39.

CARNIVAL
A teriffic show!
FEATURING
Turkel the Terrable Tiger
Lucy, the Famus Lion Tamer
Dolly Diamond, Trapeze Artest
TICKITS on Sale Now

40. Correct the spelling in the letter below. Cross out any misspelled words and write the correct word above the crossed-out word.

Agust 21

Dear Rusty,

I am the luckkiest rat in the hole world! My dream is coming true! I have just started a job as a circus cloun. I cloun arownd in shows twice a day. I am buzier than I have ever bin in my life! Come see the circus.

Love,

Lucinda

Correcting Spelling Errors

There are spelling errors in some of these book titles and movie titles. Find them. Cross out each wrong word, and write the correct word above it.

10 Best Circus Books

41. How to Be a Grate Ring Master
42. ROOLS for A LION TAMER
43. 100 Great Trapeze Triks
44. The Clown Who Cuddn't Laugh
45. Secrets of Circus Preformers
46. ELEPHENT JOKES
47. Fyre Eater's Handbook
48. Teeching Tricks to Tigers
49. Trouble on the Titerope
50. Disapearance at the Circus

10 Best Circus Movies

51. The Nife-Thrower's Mistake
52. CLOWNS on CRUCHES
53. The Invisable Circus Show
54. AKROBAT: The Movie
55. Tiger On The Lose
56. Jugglers from Owter Space
57. The Vanashing Magician
58. The Cat Who Ate the Curcus
59. Elaphants on the Tightrope
60. Mystery Abroad the Circus Train

KEEPING TRACK OF SKILLS

Student Progress Record Form 118

Class Progress Record
      (Reading, Writing, Grammar & Usage) 119

Class Progress Record
      (Words & Vocabulary, Study & Research, Spelling) 120

Good Skill Sharpeners for Language Arts 121

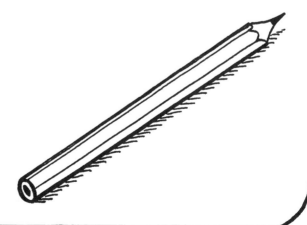

STUDENT PROGRESS RECORD — LANGUAGE SKILLS

Student Name _____

TEST DATE	READING TESTS	SCORE	COMMENTS & NEEDS
	Test # 1 Word Meanings	of 50	
	Test # 2 Literal Comprehension	of 30	
	Test # 3 Inferential & Evaluative Comprehension	of 30	
	Test # 4 Literature Skills	of 45	

TEST DATE	WRITING TESTS	SCORE	COMMENTS & NEEDS
	Test # 1 Word Choice & Word Use	of 20	
	Test # 2 Forms & Techniques	of 25	
	Test # 3 Content & Organization	of 50	
	Test # 4 Editing	of 50	
	Test # 5 Writing Process	of 30	

TEST DATE	GRAMMAR & USAGE TESTS	SCORE	COMMENTS & NEEDS
	Test # 1 Parts of Speech	of 60	
	Test # 2 Sentences	of 25	
	Test # 3 Punctuation & Capitalization	of 50	
	Test # 4 Language Usage	of 50	

TEST DATE	WORDS & VOCABULARY SKILLS TESTS	SCORE	COMMENTS & NEEDS
	Test # 1 Word Parts	of 45	
	Test # 2 Vocabulary Word Meanings	of 40	
	Test # 3 Confusing Words	of 55	

TEST DATE	STUDY & RESEARCH SKILLS TESTS	SCORE	COMMENTS & NEEDS
	Test # 1 Dictionary & Encyclopedia Skills	of 35	
	Test # 2 Reference & Information Skills	of 60	
	Test # 3 Library Skills	of 20	
	Test # 4 Study Skills	of 10	

TEST DATE	SPELLING TESTS	SCORE	COMMENTS & NEEDS
	Test # 1 Rules & Rule-Breakers	of 50	
	Test # 2 Spelling with Word Parts	of 40	
	Test # 3 Confusing & Tricky Words	of 35	
	Test # 4 Correcting Spelling Errors	of 60	

CLASS PROGRESS RECORD – LANGUAGE SKILLS
(Reading, Writing, Grammar)

Class _____ Teacher _____

READING TESTS

TEST DATE	TEST	COMMENTS ABOUT RESULTS	SKILLS NEEDING RE-TEACHING
	Test # 1 Word Meanings		
	Test # 2 Literal Comprehension		
	Test # 3 Inferential & Evaluative Comprehension		
	Test # 4 Literature Skills		

WRITING TESTS

TEST DATE	TEST	COMMENTS ABOUT RESULTS	SKILLS NEEDING RE-TEACHING
	Test # 1 Word Choice & Word Use		
	Test # 2 Forms & Techniques		
	Test # 3 Content & Organization		
	Test # 4 Editing		
	Test # 5 Writing Process		

GRAMMAR & USAGE TESTS

TEST DATE	TEST	COMMENTS ABOUT RESULTS	SKILLS NEEDING RE-TEACHING
	Test # 1 Parts of Speech		
	Test # 2 Sentences		
	Test # 3 Punctuation & Capitalization		
	Test # 4 Language Usage		

CLASS PROGRESS RECORD — LANGUAGE SKILLS
(Words & Vocabulary Skills, Study & Research Skills, Spelling)

Class _____ Teacher _____

WORDS & VOCABULARY SKILLS TESTS

TEST DATE	TEST	COMMENTS ABOUT RESULTS	SKILLS NEEDING RE-TEACHING
	Test # 1 Word Parts		
	Test # 2 Vocabulary Word Meanings		
	Test # 3 Confusing Words		

STUDY & RESEARCH SKILLS TESTS

TEST DATE	TEST	COMMENTS ABOUT RESULTS	SKILLS NEEDING RE-TEACHING
	Test # 1 Dictionary & Encyclopedia Skills		
	Test # 2 Reference & Information Skills		
	Test # 3 Library Skills		
	Test # 4 Study Skills		

SPELLING TESTS

TEST DATE	TEST	COMMENTS ABOUT RESULTS	SKILLS NEEDING RE-TEACHING
	Test # 1 Rules & Rule-Breakers		
	Test # 2 Spelling with Word Parts		
	Test # 3 Confusing & Tricky Words		
	Test # 4 Correcting Spelling Errors		

Name _____

Fourth Grade Book of Language Tests

Copyright ©2000 by Incentive Publications, Inc., Nashville, TN.

GOOD SKILL SHARPENERS FOR LANGUAGE ARTS

The tests in this book will identify student needs for practice, re-teaching or reinforcement of basic skills.

Once those areas of need are known, then what? You and your students need to find some good ways to strengthen those skills.

The BASIC/Not Boring Skills Series, published by Incentive Publications (www.incentivepublications.com), offers fourteen books to sharpen basic skills at the Grades 4–5 level. Six of these books are full of language exercises in the areas of reading, writing, grammar and language usage, study and research, vocabulary and word skills, and spelling.

The pages of these books are student-friendly, clever, and challenging—guaranteed not to be boring! They cover a wide range of skills, including the skills assessed in this book of tests. A complete checklist of skills is available at the front of each book, complete with a reference list directing you to the precise pages for polishing those skills.

TEST IN THIS BOOK 4th Grade Book of Language Tests	Pages in this Book	You will find pages to sharpen skills in these locations from the BASIC/Not Boring Skills Series, published by Incentive Publications.
Reading Test # 1 **Word Meanings**	12–17	Gr. 4–5 Reading Comprehension Gr. 4–5 Words & Vocabulary
Reading Test # 2 **Literal Comprehension**	18–23	Gr. 4–5 Reading Comprehension Gr. 4–5 Study & Research
Reading Test # 3 **Inferential & Evaluative Comprehension**	24–29	Gr. 4–5 Reading Comprehension Gr. 4–5 Study & Research
Reading Test # 4 **Literature Skills**	30–35	Gr. 4–5 Reading Comprehension
Writing Test # 1 **Word Choice & Word Use**	38–39	Gr. 4–5 Writing
Writing Test # 2 **Forms & Techniques**	40–42	Gr. 4–5 Writing
Writing Test # 3 **Content & Organization**	44–47	Gr. 4–5 Writing
Writing Test # 4 **Editing**	48–51	Gr. 4–5 Writing Gr. 4–5 Grammar & Usage
Writing Test # 5 **Writing Process**	52–59	Gr. 4–5 Writing

(continued on next page)

TEST IN THIS BOOK 4th Grade Book of Language Tests	Pages in this Book	You will find pages to sharpen skills in these locations from the BASIC/Not Boring Skills Series, published by Incentive Publications.
Grammar & Usage Test # 1 **Parts of Speech**	62–65	Gr. 4–5 Grammar & Usage
Grammar & Usage Test # 2 **Sentences**	66–67	Gr. 4–5 Grammar & Usage
Grammar & Usage Test # 3 **Punctuation & Capitalization**	68–71	Gr. 4–5 Grammar & Usage Gr. 4–5 Writing
Grammar & Usage Test # 4 **Language Usage**	72–75	Gr. 4–5 Grammar & Usage
Words & Vocabulary Skills Test # 1 **Word Parts**	78–79	Gr. 4–5 Words & Vocabulary Gr. 4–5 Spelling
Words & Vocabulary Skills Test # 2 **Vocabulary Word Meanings**	80–83	Gr. 4–5 Words & Vocabulary Gr. 4–5 Reading Comprehension
Words & Vocabulary Skills Test # 3 **Confusing Words**	84–87	Gr. 4–5 Words & Vocabulary Gr. 4–5 Spelling
Study & Research Test # 1 **Dictionary & Encyclopedia Skills**	90–93	Gr. 4–5 Study & Research
Study & Research Test # 2 **Reference & Information Skills**	94–99	Gr. 4–5 Study & Research Gr. 4–5 Reading Comprehension
Study & Research Test # 3 **Library Skills**	100–101	Gr. 4–5 Study & Research
Study & Research Test # 4 **Study Skills**	102–103	Gr. 4–5 Study & Research
Spelling Test # 1 **Rules & Rule-Breakers**	106–107	Gr. 4–5 Spelling
Spelling Test # 2 **Spelling with Word Parts**	108–109	Gr. 4–5 Spelling
Spelling Test # 3 **Confusing & Tricky Words**	110–111	Gr. 4–5 Spelling
Spelling Test # 4 **Correcting Spelling Errors**	112–116	Gr. 4–5 Spelling Gr. 4–5 Writing

SCORING GUIDES & ANSWER KEYS

Reading 124

Writing 126

Writing Process Scoring Guide 128

Grammar & Usage 130

Words & Vocabulary Skills 134

Study & Research Skills 137

Spelling 140

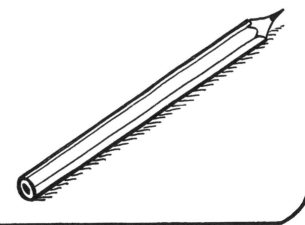

READING TESTS ANSWER KEY

Word Meanings (Test on page 12)

1. c	20. c	39. microscope
2. b	21. b	40. telephone
3. a	22. c	41. e
4. b	23. b	42. b
5. a	24. a	43. (H) Hold your horses!
6. b	25. d	44. (B) You're in the doghouse.
7. d	26. c	45. (C) You're driving me up a wall.
8. c	27. c	46. (D) Drop me a line.
9. a	28. d	47. (G) You're pulling my leg.
10. incredible	29. a	48. (A) Do it on the double.
11. acquire	30. c	49. (F) Don't try to worm your way out of it!
12. annual	31. b	50. (E) Don't horse around.
13. suitable	32. d	
14. slowly	33. solar	
15. proceed	34. visible	
16. forbidden	35. floral	
17. temporarily	36. geography	
18. b	37. aquarium	
19. d	38. pedestrian	

Literal Comprehension (Test on page 18)

1. c	17. 3
2. b	18. 3
3. c	19. no
4. b	20. d
5. c	21. SW
6. b	22. no
7. lost diamond found	23. Make sure students have placed an X at the southern edge of Lost Caves.
8. dinosaur bones	24. back
9. Pawchuck	25. front tip
10. in the mayor's burrito	26. right
11. b	27. 540
12. c	28. front
13. 6	29. McTwist
14. Grilled Ham & Fried Eggs	30. Answers will vary: U-shaped skating surface.
15. $4.55	
16. chocolate icing	

READING TESTS ANSWER KEY

Inferential & Evaluative Comprehension (Test on page 24)

1. d	11. a. E	21. a, c, d
2. a	b. C	22. d
3. b	12. O	23. d
4. b	13. F	24. c
5. c	14. O	25. no
6. b	15. X—could be true	26. yes
7. a	16. X—could be true	27. coyote
8. b	17. no X	28. lion, antelope, cheetah
9. c	18. X—could be true	29. snail, tortoise
10. a. E	19. d	30. snake, cat, rabbit
b. C	20. b, c, d	

Literature Skills (Test on page 30)

1. d
2. Alvira Rodent (or Miss Rodent)
3. Judge Will D. Side
4. a courtroom (or Curryville County Courthouse)
5. b
6. c
7. poem
8. answers will vary (probably chicken pox)
9. e
10. one of these:
    - your body will look like a road map
    - your body has more dents than a waffle iron
    - your face looks like a polka-dotted tie
11. four of these: annoying, unstopping, creeping, growing, forever, and everywhere
12. e
13. stand being stuffed, squashed, smashed, and squished into shoes *or* turned and twisted, *or* bumped and banged, *or* smothered in sweaty socks
14. walls and balls, *or* halls and malls, *or* "Not at all!" you say? Well, that's what happens to feet each day.
15. smothered in sweaty socks
16. any 4 of these:
    stuffed
    squashed
    smashed
    squished into shoes
    tied up tight
    wrapped in a ballet slipper
    smothered in sweaty socks
    crammed
17. b
18. rhythm or alliteration
19. simile
20. metaphor
21. simile
22. metaphor
23. repetition
24. personification
25. alliteration
26. idiom
27. rhyme or rhythm
28. rhyme or rhythm
29. alliteration or repetition
30. exaggeration
31. poem
32. bathtub
33. bather (cat) & rat
34. c
35. a
36. d
37. a
38. recipe or essay
39. news report
40. fable
41. joke, tall tale, myth, or imaginative story
42. argument or advertisement
43. imaginative story, tall tale, or myth
44. essay
45. poem

WRITING TESTS ANSWER KEY

Word Choice & Word Use (Test on page 38)

1. c or d
2. c
3. a
4. d
5. a
6. b
7. a
8. c
9. Answers will vary. Give credit for any reasonable answer such as: humid, slow, hot. etc.
10. Answers will vary. Give credit for any reasonable answer such as: secretive, mysterious, quiet, etc.
11. c
12. b

13–17. Circle 14, 16, 17

18. cross out: totally or whole
19. cross out: all or entire
20. cross out: Next time or when we do this again

Forms & Techniques (Test on page 40)

1–4. Answers may vary. Give credit to a student who has identified 2 or more of the choices listed.

1. C, G, H, I, and possibly A, D, E
2. A, D, and possibly C and E
3. B, F
4. A, E, and possibly G, H, and I
5. C, H, I, and possibly A and E
6. B
7. F
8. C
9. E
10. A
11. D
12. G
13. b
14. d
15. parents
16. touch/feeling
17. taste
18. smell or touch/feeling
19. 6, 7, 8, 9, 10, 11, 12, 13 (5 is optional)
20. a
21. P
22. E
23. S
24. I
25. A

WRITING TESTS ANSWER KEY

Content & Organization (Test on page 44)

To the adult:
The ten writing tasks will have varied answers. Assign 1–5 points for each, depending upon how well the student followed the directions, and how thoroughly the work is done. Do not emphasize spelling, punctuation, and capitalization too much in scoring, as it will obscure attention to the skills being examined in each task.

Answers are given below only for the one task that has a specific answer:

Task # 3:
(Students may defend a different sequence.)
1, 6, 7, 3, 4, 2, 5
or 1, 6, 7, 2, 4, 5, 3

Editing (Test on page 48)

To the adult:
Many of the ten editing tasks will have varied answers. Assign 1–5 points for each, depending upon how well the student followed the directions, and how thoroughly the work is done. Do not emphasize spelling, punctuation, and capitalization too much in scoring, except for in Task # 10, as it will obscure attention to the skills being examined in each task.
Answers are given below only for those tasks that clearly have right answers:

Task # 4:
Phrases and words that are repetitive and should be crossed out:
   a. with one wheel
   b. Either: A trio of OR three AND either: 12 p.m. OR noon
   c. Either: abundant OR large
   d. Either: In addition OR also
   e. Either: at all OR a bit
   f. Either: a true OR fact (ALSO-*really* could be an optional elimination)

Task # 5:
   a. 1, 4, 2, 5, 3
   b. 5, 1, 4, 2, 3, OR 5, 1, 3, 2, 4
   c. 2, 5, 1, 3, 4 OR 2, 5, 1, 4, 3

Task # 10:
Monday, May 15
Dear Lucy,
Did you hear what is happening? Ever since Sunday, parts of sandwiches have been showing up in odd places. A pickle and some onion slices were on my porch. A pile of sliced ham was on the stairs to the bedroom. Tomato chunks hung from my shower rod today. Salami was in my sugar bowl this morning and I found Swiss cheese in my slippers. What do you think?
Your friend,
Reggie Rat

Writing Process (Test on page 52)

Use the Writing Scoring Guide on pages 128–129 to score the student's writing sample.

Fourth Grade Book of Language Tests

WRITING PROCESS SCORING GUIDE

TRAIT	SCORE OF 5	SCORE OF 3	SCORE OF 1
CONTENT	• The writing is very clear and focused. • The main ideas and purpose stand out clearly. • Main ideas are well-supported with details and examples. • All details are relevant to the main idea. • The ideas have some freshness and insight. • The ideas fit the purpose and audience well. • The paper is interesting and holds the reader's attention.	• The writing is mostly clear and focused. • The main ideas and purpose are mostly clear. • Details and examples are used but may be somewhat limited or repetitive. • Most details are relevant to the main idea. • Some details may be off the topic. • Some ideas and details are fresh; others are ordinary. • The paper is interesting to some degree. • The ideas and content are less than precisely right for the audience and purpose.	• The writing lacks clarity and focus. • It is hard to identify the main idea. • The purpose of the writing is not evident. • Details are few, not relevant, or repetitive. • Ideas or details have little sparkle or appeal to hold the reader's attention. • The paper has not developed an idea well.
WORD CHOICE	• Writer has used strong, specific, colorful, effective, and varied words. • Words are used well to convey the ideas. • Words are well chosen to fit the content, audience, and purpose. • Writer has chosen fresh, unusual words, and/or has used words/phrases in an unusual way. • Writer has made use of figurative language, and words/phrases that create images.	• Writer has used some specific and effective words. • A good use of colorful, unusual words is attempted, but limited or overdone. • The words succeed at conveying main ideas. • The writer uses words in fresh ways sometimes, but not consistently. • The word choice is mostly suited to the content, audience, and purpose.	• There is a limited use of specific, effective, or colorful words. • Some words chosen are imprecise, misused, or repetitive. • The words do not suit the content, purpose, or audience well. • The words do not succeed at conveying the main ideas.
SENTENCES	• Sentences have a pleasing and natural flow. • When read aloud, sentences and ideas flow along smoothly from one to another. • Transitions between sentences are smooth and natural. • Sentences have varied length, structure, sound, and rhythm. • The structure of sentences focuses reader's attention on the main idea and key details. • The sentence sound and variety make the reading enjoyable. • If the writer uses dialogue, it is used correctly and effectively.	• Most of the sentences have a natural flow. • When read aloud, some sentences have a "less than fluid" sound. • Some or all transitions are awkward or repetitive. • There is some variety in sentence length, structure, sound, and rhythm; but some patterns are repetitive. • The sentences convey the main idea and details, but without much craftsmanship. • If the writer uses dialogue, it is somewhat less than fluid or effective.	• Most sentences are not fluid. • When read aloud, the writing sounds awkward or uneven. Some of the paper is confusing to read. • Transitions are not effective. • There is little variety in sentence length, structure, sound, or rhythm. • There may be incomplete or run-on sentences. • The sentence structure gets in the way of conveying content, purpose, and meaning.

A score of 4 may be given for papers that fall between 3 and 5 on a trait. A score of 2 may be given for papers that fall between 1 and 3.

WRITING PROCESS SCORING GUIDE

TRAIT	SCORE OF 5	SCORE OF 3	SCORE OF 1
ORGANIZATION	• The organization of the piece allows the main ideas and key details to be conveyed well. • The piece has a compelling beginning that catches the attention of the reader. • Ideas are developed in a clear, interesting sequence. • The piece moves along from one idea, sentence, or paragraph to another in a manner that is smooth and useful to develop the meaning. • The piece has a compelling ending that ties up the idea well and leaves the reader feeling pleased.	• Organization is recognizable, but weak or inconsistent in some places. • For the most part, the organization of the piece allows the main ideas and key details to be conveyed. • The structure seems somewhat ordinary, lacking flavor or originality. • The piece has a beginning that is not particularly inviting to the reader or not well-developed. • Some of the sequencing is confusing. • The piece does not always move along smoothly or clearly from one idea, sentence, or paragraph to another. • The piece has a clear ending, but it is somewhat dull or underdeveloped, or does not adequately tie up the piece.	• The piece lacks clear organization. • For the most part, the lack of good organization gets in the way of the conveyance of the main ideas and key details. • The piece does not have a clear beginning or ending. • Ideas are not developed in any clear sequence, or the sequence is distracting. • The piece does not move along smoothly from one sentence or paragraph to another. • Important ideas or details seem to be missing or out of place. • The piece leaves the reader feeling confused.
VOICE	• The writer has left a personal stamp on the piece. A reader knows there is a person behind the writing. • It is clear that the writer knows what audience and purpose he/she is reaching. • The writer engages the audience. • The writer shows passion, commitment, originality, and honesty in conveying the message. • The voice used (level of personal closeness) is appropriate for the purpose of the piece.	• The writer has left a personal stamp on the piece, but this is not as strong or consistent as it might be. The reader is not always sure of the writer's presence. • It is not always clear that the writer knows his/her audience and purpose. • The writer engages the audience some, but not all of the time. • The writer shows some passion, commitment, originality, and honesty in conveying the message, but this is inconsistent.	• The writer has not left any personal stamp on the piece. The writing feels detached. • There is little sense that the writer is speaking to the audience or clearly knows the purpose of the writing. • There is little or no engagement of the audience. • The writer shows little or no passion, commitment, originality, and honesty in conveying the message.
CONVENTIONS	• There is clear control of capitalization, punctuation, spelling, and paragraphing. • There is consistent use of correct grammar and language usage. • The strong use of conventions strengthens the communication of the work's meaning. • The piece needs little editing/revision.	• There is some control of capitalization, punctuation, spelling, and paragraphing. • There is inconsistent use of correct grammar and language usage. • The uneven use of conventions sometimes interferes with the meaning. • The piece needs much editing/revision.	• There is poor control of capitalization, punctuation, spelling, and paragraphing. • There is a lack of correct grammar and language usage. • Poor use of conventions obscures meaning. • There are multiple errors; the piece needs extensive editing/revision.

A score of 4 may be given for papers that fall between 3 and 5 on a trait. A score of 2 may be given for papers that fall between 1 and 3.

GRAMMAR & USAGE ANSWER KEY

Parts of Speech (Test on page 62)

1. N
2. AD
3. V
4. AJ
5. AJ
6. AJ
7. N
8. AD
9. V
10. N
11. wandered
12. Four, tired, lost, dark
13. hopelessly
14. hikers, woods
15. raccoons, pizza, kitchen, chance, cabin
16. Saturday, Camp Lookout, Elmo
17. our, it, us
18. watches
19. calves
20. potatoes
21. geese
22. surprises
23. canoes
24. backpacks
25. donkeys
26. foxes
27. deer
28. mouse
29. friend
30. box
31. child
32. leaf
33. man
34. ruby
35. monkey
36. radio
37. campfire
38. boat's oars
39. campers' tent
40. owl's hoots
41. bears' teeth
42. flashlight's batteries
43. raccoon's tail
44. paddled
45. screeching
46. stopped
47. swam
48. burns or will burn
49. eat
50. dove
51. fed
52. struck
53. told
54. watch
55. built
56. A, B
57. A, B
58. A, B
59. B, A
60. A, B

GRAMMAR & USAGE ANSWER KEY

Sentences (Test on page 66)

1. F
2. R
3. C
4. F
5. R
6. C
7. C (H is optional)
8. B, E (H is optional)
9. D, F
10. A, G
11. Cold, shivering campers
12. the crackling fire
13. The orange flames
14. opened the bag of plump marshmallows
15. fell into the fire
16. burned the last batch of marshmallows
17. campers
18. water
19. swimmers
20. race
21. love
22. beat

23–25. Answers may vary from those shown. Make sure student has followed directions accurately.

23. Someone screamed, "Help!" The lifeguard ran into the water. OR Someone screamed, "Help!" and the lifeguard ran into the water.

24. The lifeguard moved so fast that she got to the swimmer in seconds. OR The lifeguard moved so fast. She got to the swimmer in seconds.

25. A shark was spotted and the swimmers raced for safety. OR, When a shark was spotted, the swimmers raced for safety. OR The swimmers raced for safety when a shark was spotted.

GRAMMAR & USAGE ANSWER KEY

Punctuation & Capitalization (Test on page 68)

1. Corrected letter:

   Saturday, August 4

   Dear Mr. and Mrs. Johnson,

   Greetings to you from the shores of Lake Lookout! Your son and his cabin mates are having a great time here in Wisconsin. On Monday through Friday, the campers swim, hike, and practice boating, sailing, and archery. Our French cook makes great meals. Today, they had grilled Swiss cheese sandwiches. Last Monday, the kids watched a good movie about camping in Australia and heard some unusual English ghost stories. Everyone is having fun.

   Sincerely,

   Counselor Caspian Cat

2. Circle: camps, united, states, atlantic, ocean, pacific, ocean, june, august
3. c
4. Correct by capitalizing fun, but, harmless, camp, pranks
5. Correct
6. Correct
7. Correct by capitalizing woods
8. Correct by capitalizing ghost and stories
9. Correct
10. they will
11. will not
12. we would or we had
13. was not
14. you have
15. wouldn't
16. they've
17. I'd
18. you'll
19. aren't
20. a
21. Correctly punctuated sentences are: A, D, E, H, and I.
22. c
23. b
24. Trail to Lookout Campground is to the right.
25. Mount Grizzly is 4300 feet high.
26. HORSE STABLES are 1 mile this way.
27. Follow Cool Springs Trail to the Camp Lookout Archery Range (optional capitalization on Archery and Range)
28. Follow this trail east to good food at the Paradise Lake Dining Hall.
29. All swimmers must shower before entering the pool.
30. The swimming pool is this way.
31. Swimming pool hours are 10 to 5.
32. Tennis courts must be reserved ahead of time.

GRAMMAR & USAGE ANSWER KEY

Language Usage (Test on page 72)

1. were
2. have
3. are
4. listen
5. pack
6. snuggle
7. crash
8. hide
9. their
10. them
11. hers
12. it
13. her
14. c
15. a
16. them
17. me
18. We
19. she
20. I
21. d
22. a
23. Correct use of negatives: Circle sentences B, C, D, E, and G
24. replace *learn* with *teach*
25. Cross out *he*
26. Replace *sit* with *set*
27. Replace *don't* with *doesn't*
28. Replace *well* with *good*
29. Replace *of* with *have*
30. Replace *set* with *sit*
31. Replace *leave* with *let*
32. Replace *of* with *have*
33. Cross out *it*
34. Replace *Let* with *Leave*
35. Replace *good* with *well*
36. their
37. your
38. There
39. its
40. whole
41. meat
42. would
43. our
44. noisier
45. scariest
46. latest
47. hungrier
48. more often
49. best
50. worse

WORDS & VOCABULARY SKILLS ANSWER KEY

Word Parts (Test on page 78)

1. antibiotic
2. semicircle
3. mistake
4. precook
5. centimeter
6. transfer
7. miniature
8. rewrite
9. substandard
10. pre
11. re
12. dis
13. mini
14. bi
15. trans
16. super
17. mid
18. non
19. sub
20. im
21. semi
22. mis
23. ar
24. ful
25. lets
26. er
27. less
28. en
29. ward
30. ly
31. ous
32. or
33. I
34. D
35. B
36. A
37. E
38. G
39. C
40. F
41. H
42. J
43. campfire, seaside, surfboard
44. sunshine, seasick, starfish, sunstroke
45. seaweed, sailboat, shipwreck, underwater

WORDS & VOCABULARY SKILLS ANSWER KEY

Vocabulary Word Meanings (Test on page 80)

1. a buoy	21. weak
2. on a ship	22. insult
3. on a dancer	23. important
4. find facts in it	24. endanger
5. applaud	25. approval
6. enemy	26. daring
7. bandit	27. squelch
8. annual	28. scorching
9. penalize	29. meandered
10. valiant	30. irate
11. previous	31. dazzling
12. weird	32. continue
13. hurry	33. fragile
14. prompt	34. accurate
15. brag	35. stout
16. ridiculous	36. combine
17. expert	37. impolite
18. survive	38. quarter
19. manual	39. pupil
20. vacant	40. row

WORDS & VOCABULARY SKILLS ANSWER KEY

Confusing Words (Test on page 84)

1. leak
2. rays
3. through
4. pail
5. stares
6. clothes
7. patience
8. fourth, hole
9. eight
10. sell
11. cents
12. for
13. beach
14. sail
15. not
16. prints
17. weather
18. through
19. insured
20. affect
21. except
22. infested
23. advice
24. Lunar
25. anchor
26. majority
27. vertical
28. terrestrial
29. sailing
30. lobster
31. irresistible
32. mare
33. memory
34. waffle
35. cabbage
36. tortilla
37. sauerkraut
38. molasses
39. frankfurter
40. doughnut
41. J
42. C
43. A
44. I
45. F
46. H
47. D
48. E
49. G
50. B
51. water
52. mice
53. Swim
54. safe or safety
55. judge or lawyer

STUDY & RESEARCH SKILLS ANSWER KEY

Dictionary & Encyclopedia Skills (Test on page 90)

1. 4, 2, 1, 3, 5	19. yes
2. c	20. no
3. a	21. Taiwan and table tennis
4. 4, 3, 2, 1	22. Saturn
5. 2, 1, 3, 4	23. Kansas
6. 3, 1, 4, 2, 5	24. orchestra
7. 2, 4, 1, 3	25. detectives
8. no	26. muscular pain
9. 910	27. 3
10. yes	28. New Latin
11. no	29. 3
12. yes	30. mysteries
13. 911	31. ships, boats, planes
14. no	32. 440,000 square miles
15. yes	33. Atlantic
16. yes	34. 1918
17. no	35. answers will vary: alien abductions, unknown force pulling objects into a hole in the sky
18. yes	

STUDY & RESEARCH SKILLS ANSWER KEY

Reference & Information Skills (Test on page 94)

1. G
2. J
3. H
4. D
5. E
6. B
7. A
8. F
9. I
10. D or L
11. I or K
12. D
13. E or I
14. J or I
15. J or I
16. C
17. A or I
18. B or I
19. F
20. L or D
21. H
22. M or I
23. title page
24. table of contents
25. glossary
26. copyright page
27. index
28. 37–41
29. 1
30. 4
31. 8–11 (or Glossary)
32. 80–99
33. 73–79
34. 4 pages
35. 31–36
36. 37–41
37. 73–79
38. 40–41
39. 62–69
40. 12–29
41. 8–11
42. 61–99
43. B
44. D
45. Curious County Highway
46. east
47. Mystery Town
48. Snoop Road
49. Clueless Parkway and Curious County Highway
50. 8 hours, 40 minutes
51. 30 minutes
52. suspect is found
53. 2 hours, 20 minutes
54. D. D. Scover
55. D. D. Scover
56. 10
57. food items
58. 10
59. May
60. 3

STUDY & RESEARCH SKILLS ANSWER KEY

Library Skills (Test on page 100)

1. C-B-A
2. C
3. C
4. A
5. B
6. B
7. Erwin & Sons
8. Funniest Sports Mistakes
9. A
10. 1996
11. G. Gordon Brown
12. 140
13. F
14. B
15. N
16. N
17. N
18. F
19. N
20. B

Study Skills (Test on page 102)

1. A, B, D, E, and G
2. "What a nasty rain!"
3. at the zoo
4. that she was imagining it
5. Answers will vary. Answer should be something close to this idea: Gigi's house was mysteriously clean each morning and she thought the rats in her new painting were responsible.
6. C, E, and F
7. A
8. III A
9. II D
10. I B

SPELLING ANSWER KEY

Rules & Rule-Breakers (Test on page 106)

1. grief
2. believe
3. friend
4. receive
5. piece
6. sleigh
7. weight
8. neighbor
9. ceiling
10. necessary
11. caterpillar
12. embarrass
13. scissors
14. committee
15. bananas
16. whistled
17. circles
18. gymnastic
19. caramel
20. sugar
21. quickly
22. potato
23. child
24. mouse
25. city
26. fox
27. gorilla
28. geese
29. ponies
30. scarves
31. donkeys
32. echoes
33. gentlemen
34. dragonfly, flashlight
35. bedspread
36. seashell
37. married
38. watched
39. went
40. forgot
41. argued
42. brought
43. sang
44. applied
45. truly
46. science
47. height
48. solos
49. weird
50. foreign

SPELLING ANSWER KEY

Spelling With Word Parts (Test on page 108)

1. prepare
2. submarine
3. impolite
4. correct
5. correct
6. nonsense
7. antibiotic
8. transfer
9. correct
10. correct
11. friendliness
12. wonderful
13. correct
14. dangerous
15. gravity
16. pianist
17. musical
18. appearance
19. laboratory
20. mountainous
21. difference
22. dentistry
23. misspell
24. disapprove
25. hurried
26. running
27. hoping
28. praising
29. echoed
30. clapping
31. excitement
32. candle
33. vacation
34. surprise
35. possible
36. favorite
37. travel
38. chocolate
39. garbage
40. nervous

SPELLING ANSWER KEY

Confusing & Tricky Words (Test on page 110)

1. knot, comb, honor, ghost, knife, wrinkle, wreath, fudge, knee
2. mosquito
3. correct
4. octopus
5. diamond
6. correct
7. pajamas
8. correct
9. correct
10. ai
11. ie
12. oi
13. ou
14. eo
15. ea
16. mathematics, restaurant, caterpillar, disappointment
17. b
18. a
19. c
20. b
21. c
22. a
23. b
24. b
25. c
26. a
27. aloud
28. thrown
29. ceiling
30. sent
31. diary
32. caller
33. except
34. angles
35. cartoon

SPELLING ANSWER KEY

Correcting Spelling Errors (Test on page 112)

1. California
2. Thursday
3. Earth
4. Miami
5. Mexico
6. yes
7. no
8. no
9. yes
10. no
11. yes
12. sandwich
13. twelfth
14. opposite
15. cocoon
16. serious
17. enough
18. elephant, laughter, trapeze, circus, weird, entertain
19. terrific
20. impossible
21. stomach
22. exercise
23. realize
24. tongue
25. biscuit
26. 4

(Order may vary for answers 27–32)
27. juggler
28. balloon
29. doctor
30. trouble
31. headache
32. lucky

33. often
34. numb
35. handling
36. frightened
37. escape
38. planet, elephants, wrestling, gorillas, animal
39. terrific, terrible, famous, artist, tickets
40. August, luckiest, whole, clown, clown, around, busier, been
41. Great
42. Rules
43. Tricks
44. Couldn't
45. Performers
46. Elephant
47. Fire
48. Teaching
49. Tightrope
50. Disappearance
51. Knife
52. Crutches
53. Invisible
54. Acrobat
55. Loose
56. Outer
57. Vanishing
58. Circus
59. Elephants
60. Aboard